ADDITION & SUBTRACTION
Kindergarten
MATH WORKBOOK

100 Fun Activities
to Build Core Math Skills
with Focused Practice

Naoya Imanishi, MEd

Illustrated by Gareth Williams

A **Brightly** Book
Z KIDS · NEW YORK

Zeitgeist™ is a trademark of Penguin Random House LLC
ISBN: 9780593690123

Illustrations by Gareth Williams
Book design by Katy Brown
Author photograph © by Jennifer Lazaro
Edited by Erin Nelson

Manufactured in China
1st Printing

CONTENTS

Introduction
A NOTE TO GROWN-UPS

Thank you, parents, caregivers, educators, for choosing *Addition & Subtraction Kindergarten Math Workbook*, an additional (pun intended) activity book to *Complete Kindergarten Math Workbook*. This book focuses on developing conceptual understanding of addition and subtraction while also providing opportunities for young mathematicians to develop memorization skills and fact fluency.

As an educator since 2000, I have enjoyed developing math lessons to help students succeed. I have worked as an elementary school teacher and a math coach, as well as a facilitator of Cognitively Guided Instruction with the UCLA Mathematics Project.

This book is organized by chapters and progresses in difficulty. Your child may need assistance in reading the instructions or help in understanding concepts, and that's okay. Allow plenty of time for them to think (they should be doing the math, not you). The Common Core State Standards for Mathematical Practice address perseverance and justifying one's thinking. With struggle comes learning. However, we understand all learners vary, so if skipping a problem and returning to it later works better, by all means.

You can best engage with your kindergartner by clarifying, guiding, and extending questions like, "What makes that number work there?" "What patterns do you notice?" or "Can you solve it another way?" When solving math problems, you can encourage your child to use various manipulatives—counters, blocks, and yes, their fingers—to support their counting and calculating strategies.

Ultimately, my goal is to have your child love math. I hope this book will serve as a small stepping stone toward that goal.

HOW TO USE THIS BOOK

Since conceptual understanding of addition and subtraction go hand in hand, it is not absolutely necessary to complete the pages of this book in order. If you want to have your child do the first five pages of chapter 2 for addition and then the first five pages of chapter 3 in subtraction, that's perfectly fine. The problems within the chapters, however, do increase in difficulty, so choosing random pages out of order may or may not work for your child.

Grown-ups, several problems have multiple solution paths. Please take the time to read the directions to your child and make sure they understand the task at hand. It is important to note that for the story problems, your child may use addition to solve it when you may see it as a subtraction problem. Try your best to build on what your child is doing to solve it, not so much having them do it your way. It will make more sense to them.

While some problems in this book may seem beyond the kindergarten level, the purpose is to serve as a foundation for strong conceptual understanding in mathematics. Happy exploring!

CHAPTER 1

WARM-UP: READY FOR ANYTHING!

This chapter is about the numbers 0 (zero) to 20 (twenty). Let's practice counting, writing, and recognizing those numbers.

Make it fun and count things around the house—your toys, pens, socks, anything! If you can count past 20, do you notice any patterns after every decade (10 numbers)? Try a little bit every day and see if you can get to 100!

WRITING NUMBERS

Trace each **number**. Then circle the **group** that matches the **amount**.

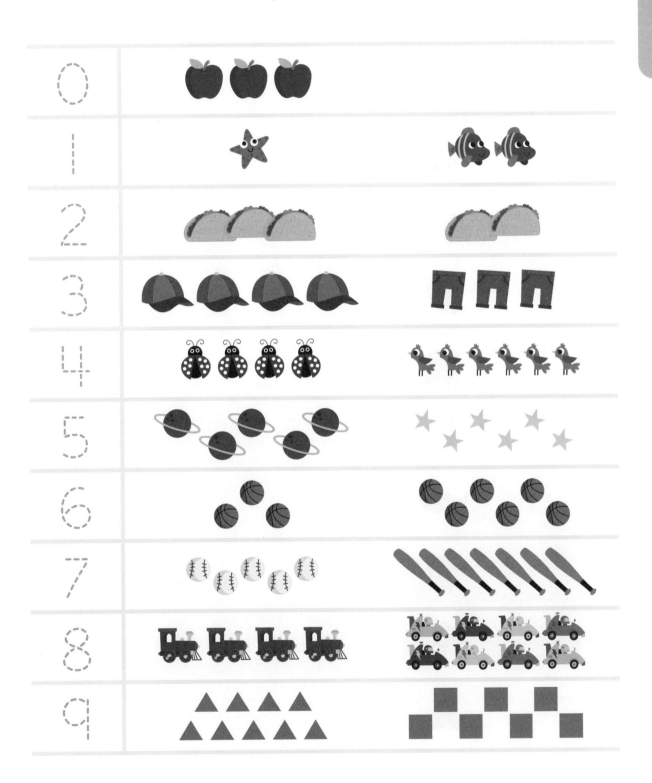

ACTIVITY 2 · NUMBER IDENTIFICATION

WRITE HOW MANY

Trace each number. Then copy the image to draw that many items.

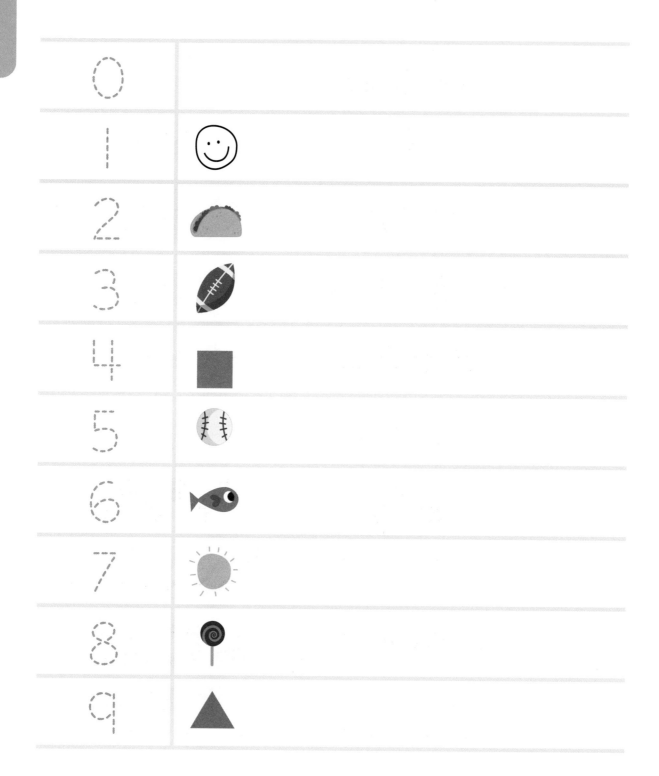

NUMBER NAMES

Trace the name for each number.

0

Zero

1

One

2

Two

3

Three

4

Four

ACTIVITY 4 · NUMBER IDENTIFICATION

NAME THIS NUMBER

Trace the name for each number.

5

Five

6

Six

7

Seven

8

Eight

9

Nine

FIND FLOR'S FLOWERS

Count the flowers and write the total number in the flower box.

ACTIVITY 6 · COUNTING

COUNT CATALINA'S CATS

Count the cats and write the total number of each cat cluster.

ACTIVITY 7 · NUMBER SEQUENCING

WRITE THE MISSING NUMBER

Write the missing number in the carts so the numbers are in order. Hint: Counting in order out loud will help you.

ACTIVITY 8 • NUMBER SEQUENCING

WHAT NUMBER IS MISSING?

Help Hana put her horses in order. Circle the correct number for the blank horse.

6   8

9   5
7

11   12

13   14
3

15   17

18   16
14

18   19

10   7
20

ACTIVITY 9 · IDENTIFYING LIKE NUMBERS

SAME SEASHELLS

Count the seashells in each box. Circle a group
of seashells that makes the same total.

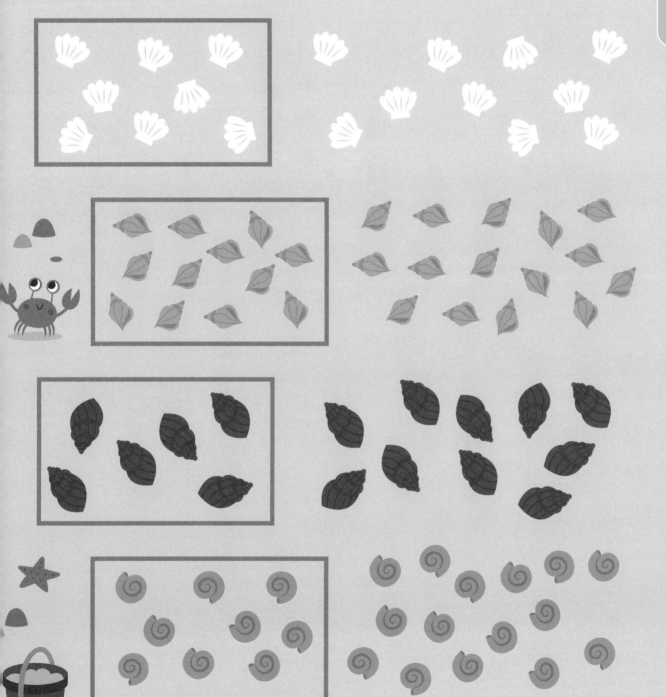

15

ACTIVITY 10 · IDENTIFYING LIKE NUMBERS

SAME STARS

Help Satoru find matching numbers of stars. Draw a line from one group of stars to another group with the same number of stars.

TALLY UP FARM

Draw tally marks for each number of animals shown.

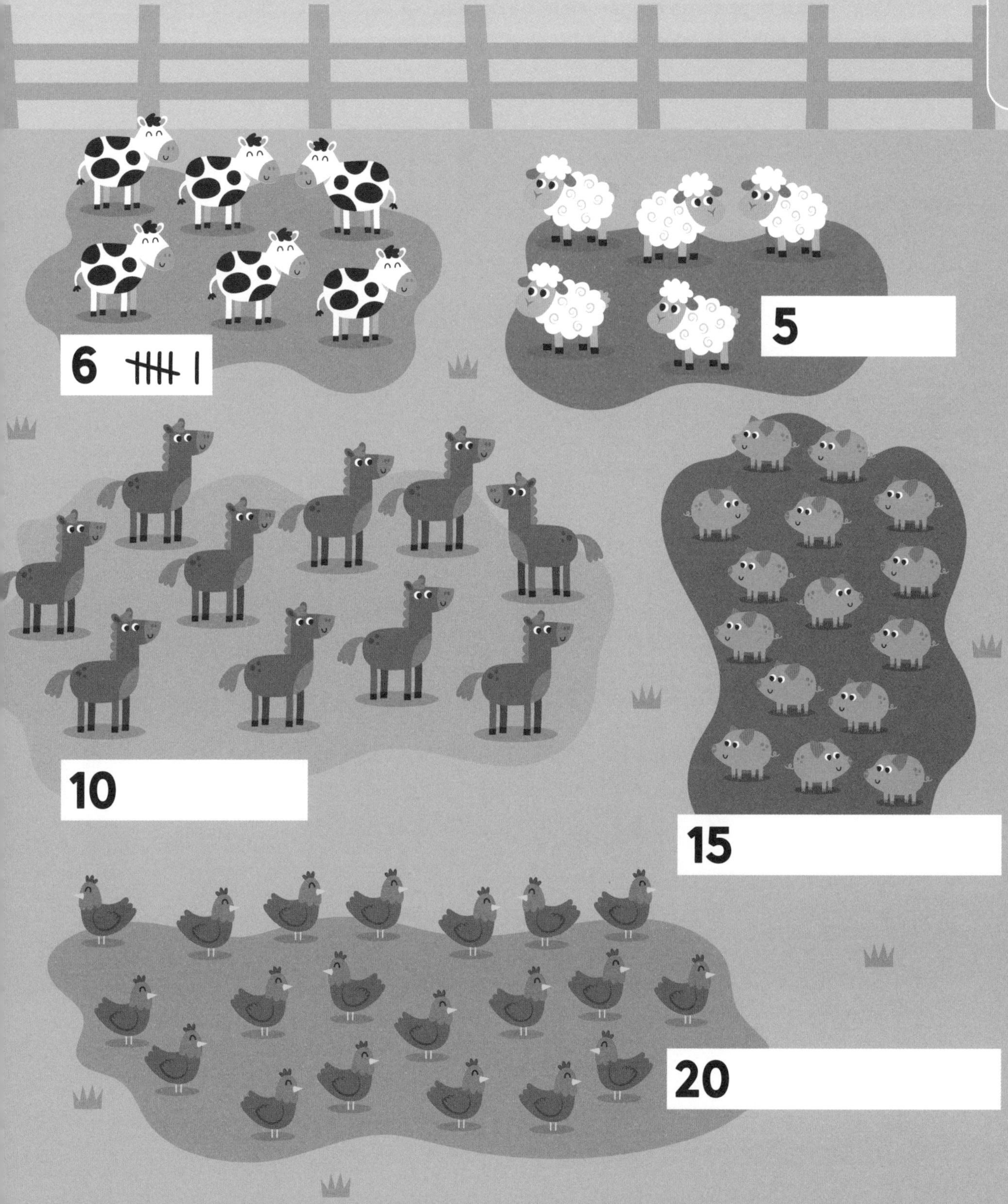

6 〲〲〲〲 〲 I

5

10

15

20

ACTIVITY 12 · IDENTIFYING ZERO

ZERO THE HERO

Zero is an important number. By itself it means there is nothing, but zero can help other numbers become bigger! Help each number become bigger by writing in the zeroes for every number set.

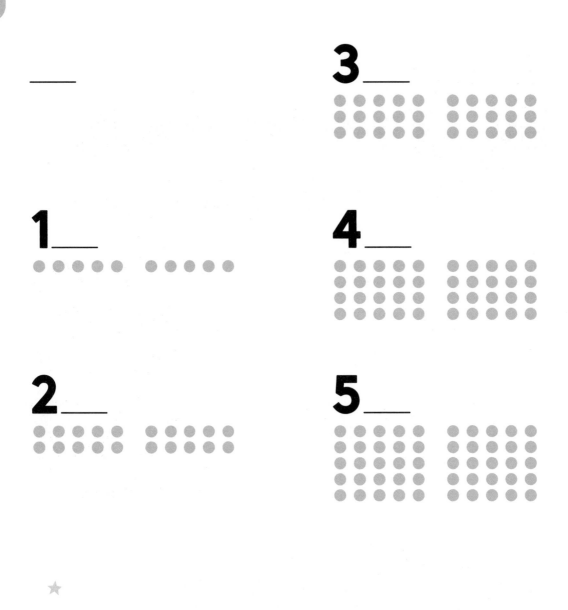

COUNTING MY ALPHABET SOUP

Count how many times you see each letter in the bowl. Circle the letters as you count. Then write each total in the boxes below.

ACTIVITY 14 · COUNTING/COMBINING

TIME FOR 10

Circle groups of 10 bugs. The groups don't have to be all the same bug. Answers will vary.

How many groups of 10 did you make? _____

MAKE A TEN FRAME

Complete the ten frames. Write the number of dots you drew that helped to make 10.

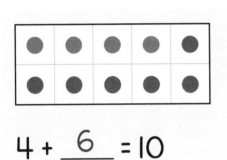

4 + __6__ = 10

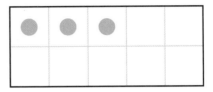

3 + _____ = 10

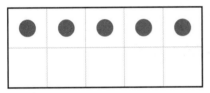

5 + _____ = 10

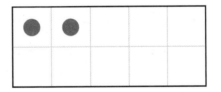

2 + _____ = 10

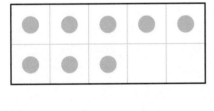

8 + _____ = 10

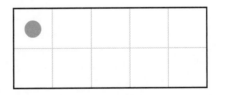

1 + _____ = 10

ADDING IT UP

In chapter 2, you'll count two numbers and put them together, like two pieces of bread in a sandwich. In adding, or **addition**, think of it as two parts making a whole.

When you **add** numbers up, you are making bigger numbers! Can you find things in your home that you can add up?

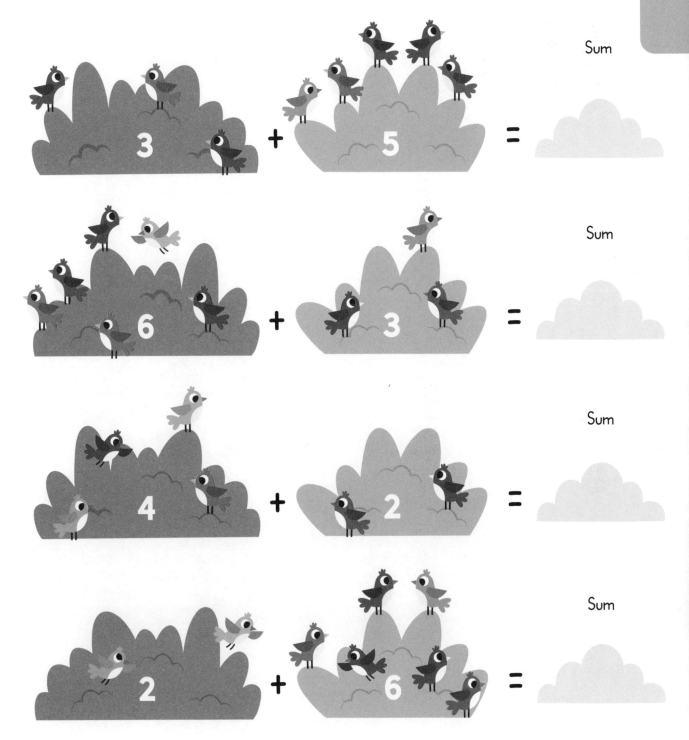

ACTIVITY 16 · FIND THE SUM

SUM THING IS UP

When you count up the total number of things, you are finding the **sum**! Find the sum of each set of birds and write the number in the cloud.

3 + 5 = Sum

6 + 3 = Sum

4 + 2 = Sum

2 + 6 = Sum

ACTIVITY 17 • FIND THE SUM

SPORTY SUMS

Help Sari's Sports Store count up their balls. Write each sum in the box.

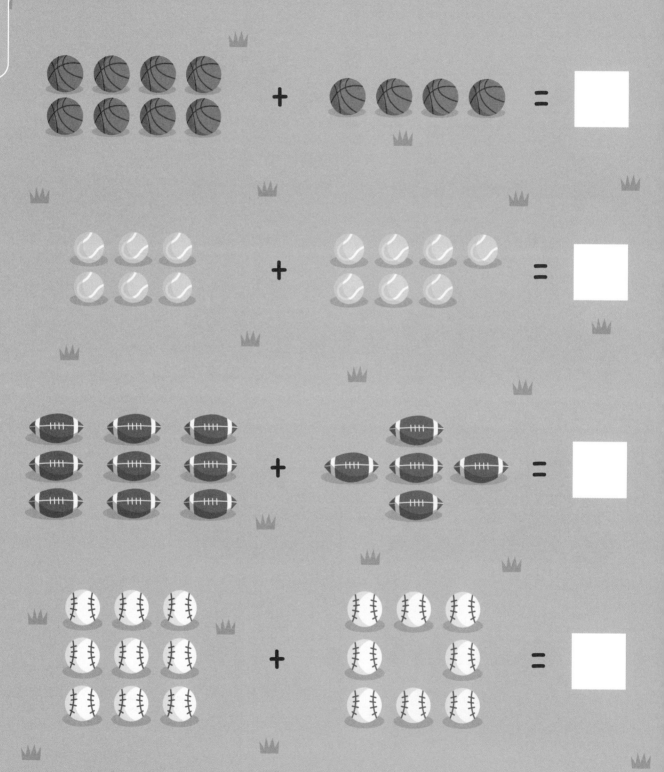

ACTIVITY 18 • FIND THE SUM

BUDDY'S BONE-BONES

Every day, Buddy hides some bones in the morning and some bones at night in his backyard. Help him count all the bones he hid each day.

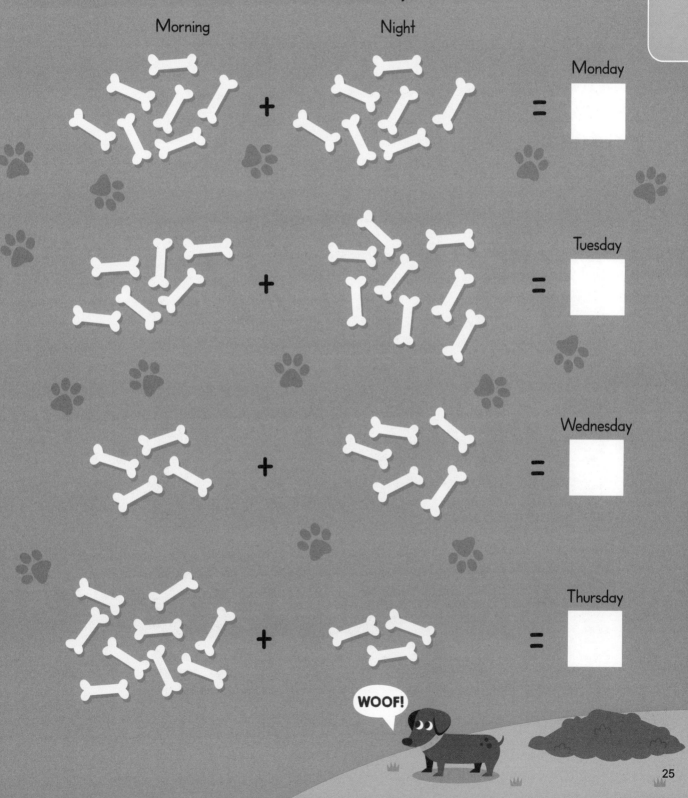

Morning   Night

Monday
Tuesday
Wednesday
Thursday

WOOF!

ACTIVITY 19 · FIND THE SUM

GROCERY GRAB

Glennard is going grocery shopping. Help him count his groceries!

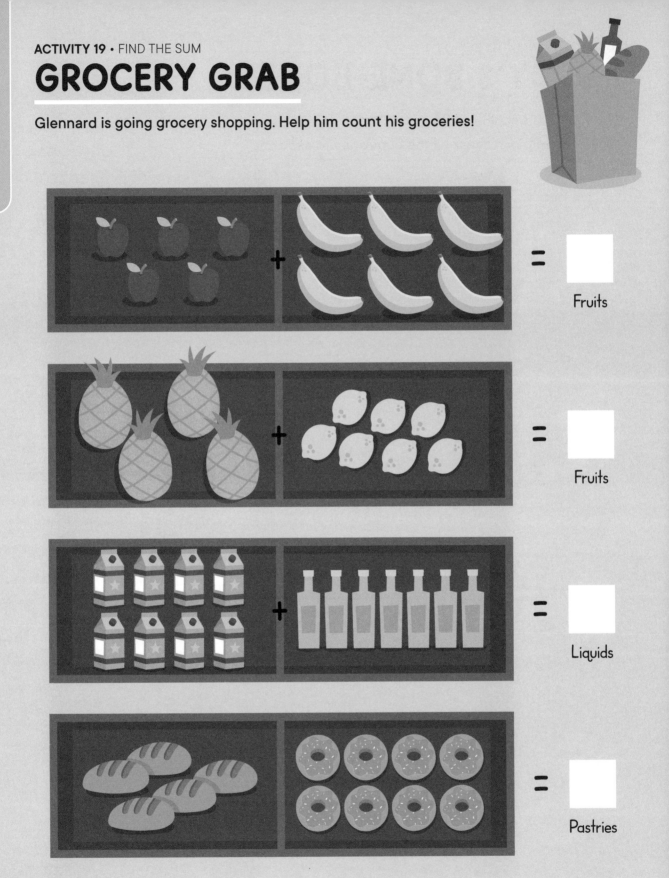

= [ ] Fruits

= [ ] Fruits

= [ ] Liquids

= [ ] Pastries

ACTIVITY 20 • NUMBER SENTENCES

THOSE ARE SUM SEEDS!

Number sentences help us show how we are counting things. Count the seeds on each watermelon slice and write a number sentence to show the sum.

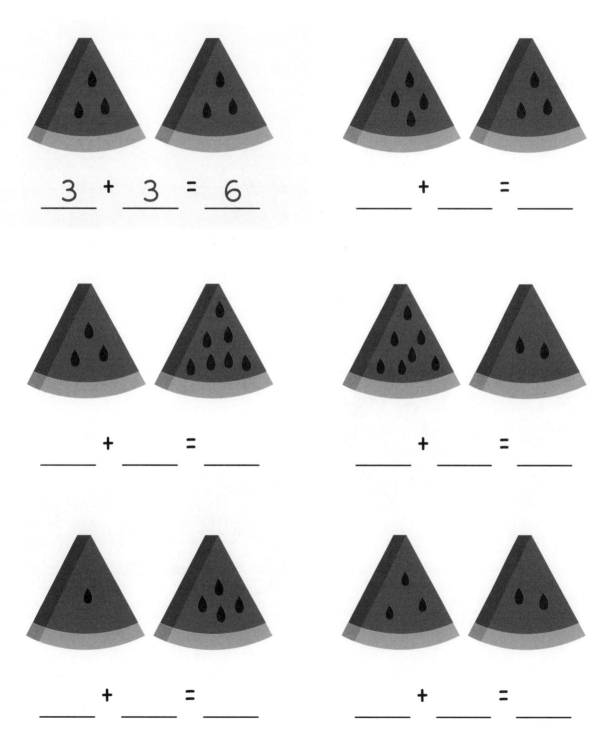

3 + 3 = 6

____ + ____ = ____

____ + ____ = ____

____ + ____ = ____

____ + ____ = ____

____ + ____ = ____

ACTIVITY 21 · NUMBER SENTENCES

POCKET PENNIES

Peyton has pennies in her pockets. Write a number sentence to show how many pennies she has in each pair of pockets.

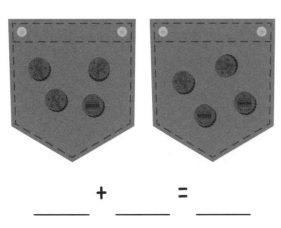

_____ + _____ = _____

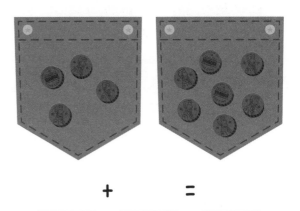

_____ + _____ = _____

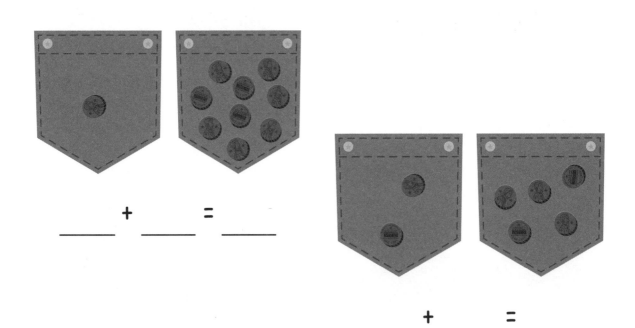

_____ + _____ = _____

_____ + _____ = _____

ACTIVITY 22 · NUMBER SENTENCES

LET IT BEE

Binh has a bee farm. Help him count the bees and write a number sentence under each beehive box.

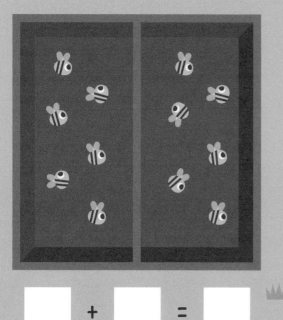

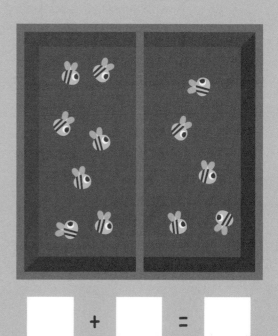

☐ + ☐ = ☐

☐ + ☐ = ☐

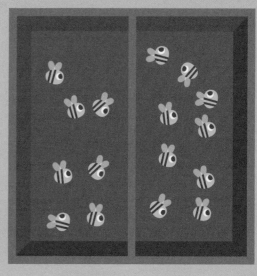

☐ + ☐ = ☐

☐ + ☐ = ☐

ACTIVITY 23 • NUMBER SENTENCES

PETTING ZOO

The numbers you add in an addition number sentence are called **addends**.
For each group of animals, circle the two different types. Count how many there
are of each type then write the addends in a number sentence to find the sum.

ACTIVITY 24 • NUMBER SENTENCES

LUNCH COUNT

Help the cafeteria crew add how many students are at each table. Write the number sentence for each table. Then circle the table with the largest number of students.

_____ + _____ = _____

_____ + _____ = _____

_____ + _____ = _____

ACTIVITY 25 • NUMBER SENTENCES

THEODORE'S DOORS

Theodore's house has lots of interesting doors with shapes of different colors and sizes on them. Find the different types of shapes you see on each door. Then write an addition **equation** to show the total.

_____ + _____ = _____

_____ + _____ = _____

_____ + _____ = _____

_____ + _____ = _____

32

ACTIVITY 26 • NUMBER SENTENCES

YUKI'S KITCHEN

Yuki has lots of cooking tools. Find the sum of some of the tools in her kitchen.

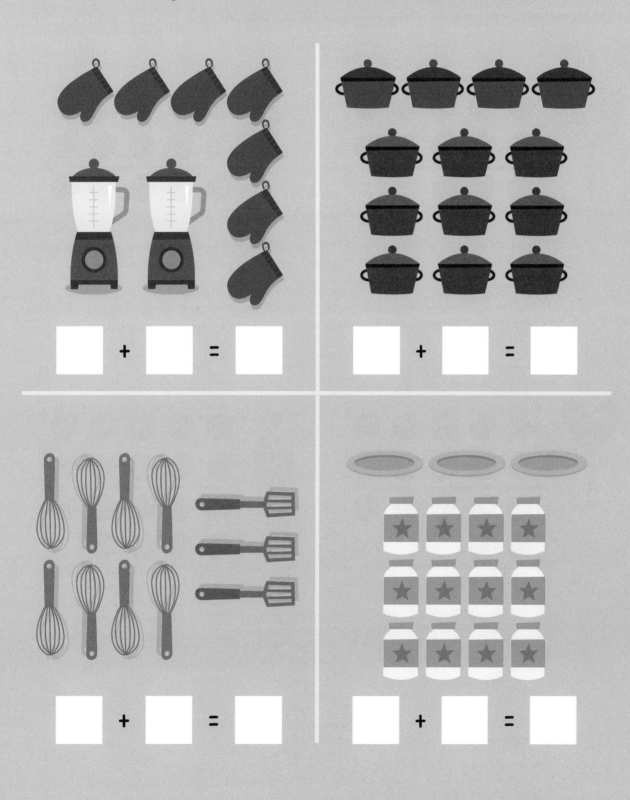

ACTIVITY 27 • NUMBER SENTENCES

CAROLYN'S CANDY SHOP

Carolyn is selling candy. Help her add up the coins above and below the center line to find the cost of each candy. Write the equation to show the sum.

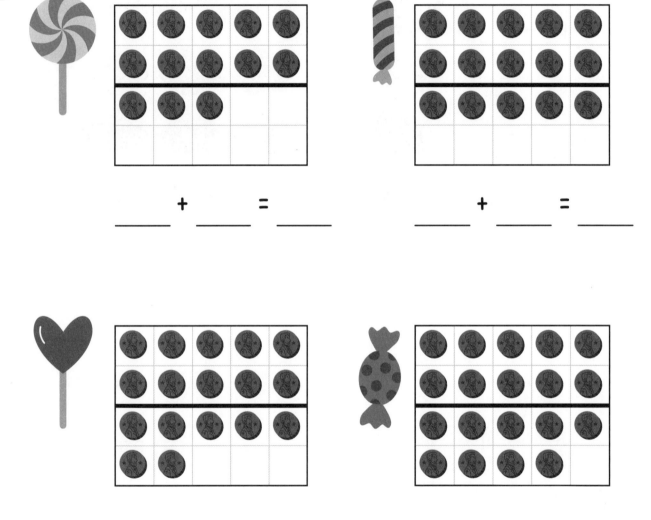

____ + ____ = ____

____ + ____ = ____

____ + ____ = ____

____ + ____ = ____

Note to grown-ups: *Encourage groupings of 10, but if your child sees another combination of numbers to find the sum, go with it!*

34

ACTIVITY 28 • FACT FAMILIES

DOTS ON DICE

Fact families are related number sentences that use the same numbers. Alma is rolling dice. For each pair of dice, draw in the number of dots Alma needs to make the number at the top.

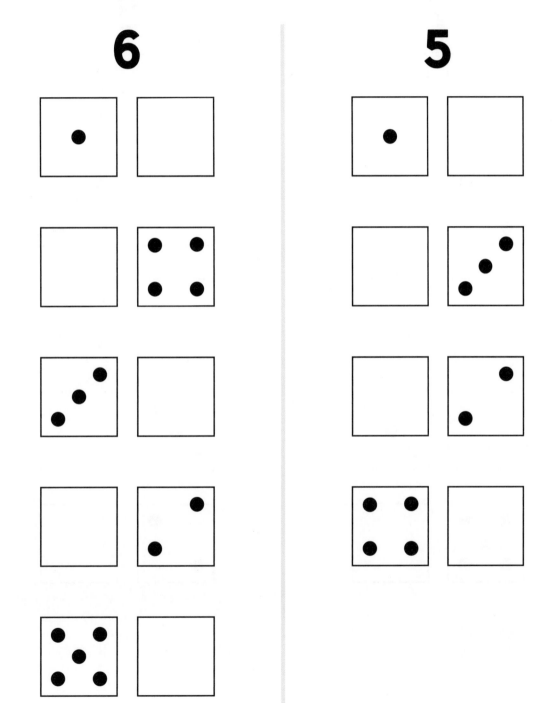

ACTIVITY 29 • FACT FAMILIES

MORE DOTS ON DICE

For each pair of dice, draw in the number of dots needed to make the number at the top.

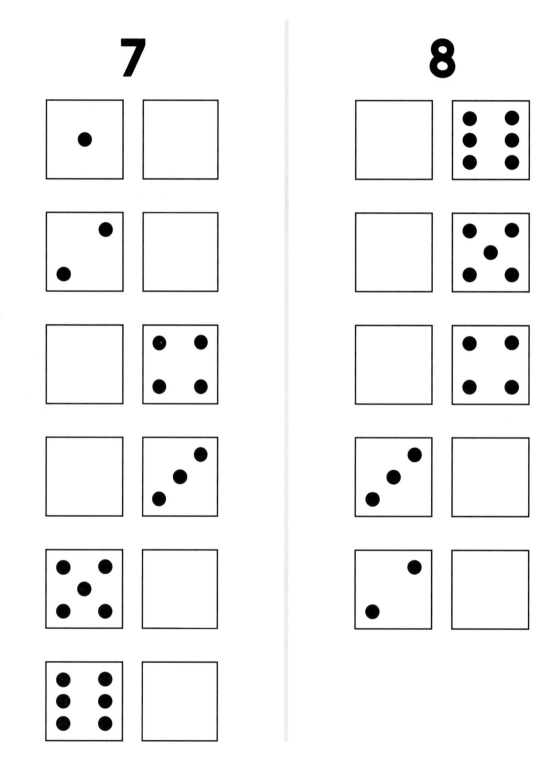

ACTIVITY 30 • FACT FAMILIES

TIME FOR TENS

Tak is making groups of tens. Help him by adding more dots to the ten frames, then write the equation that makes 10!

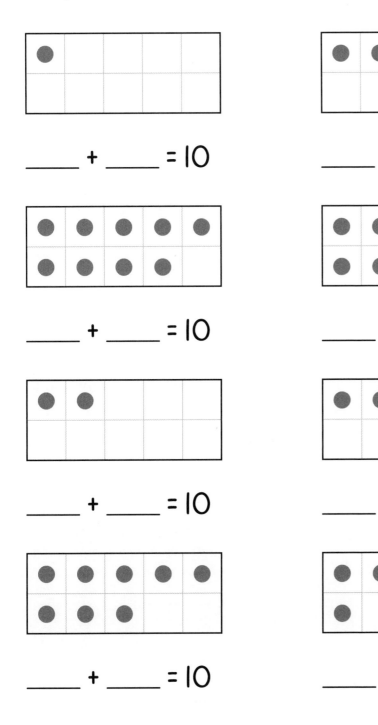

_____ + _____ = 10

_____ + _____ = 10

_____ + _____ = 10

_____ + _____ = 10

_____ + _____ = 10

_____ + _____ = 10

_____ + _____ = 10

_____ + _____ = 10

ACTIVITY 31 • FACT FAMILIES

WHAT PATTERN DO YOU SEE?

First count the number of blocks in each set. Then tell a grown-up a pattern you notice in the green and orange blocks. What pattern do you see in the blue and yellow blocks? How about the pink and red blocks?

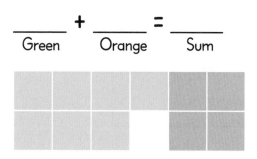

_____ + _____ = _____
Green   Orange   Sum

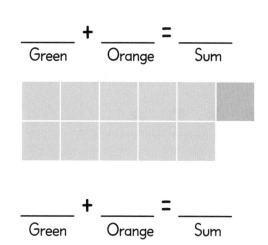

_____ + _____ = _____
Green   Orange   Sum

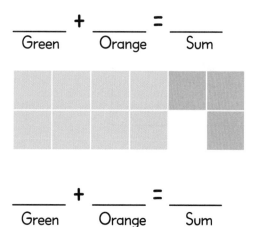

_____ + _____ = _____
Green   Orange   Sum

_____ + _____ = _____
Green   Orange   Sum

_____ + _____ = _____
Green   Orange   Sum

Note to grown-ups: It's okay if your child sees a cluster different from the answer key, as long as they can justify and make connections with the number sets. For example, rather than 6 + 6, they may say, "3 + 3, and then 3 + 3 again," or "3 + 3 + 3 + 3."

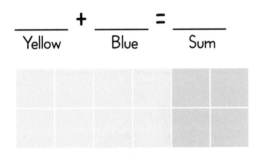

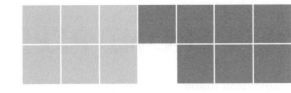

_____ + _____ = _____
Yellow   Blue   Sum

_____ + _____ = _____
Pink   Red   Sum

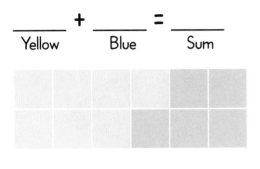

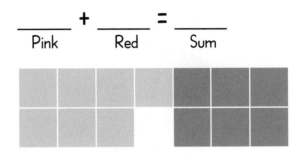

_____ + _____ = _____
Yellow   Blue   Sum

_____ + _____ = _____
Pink   Red   Sum

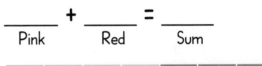

_____ + _____ = _____
Yellow   Blue   Sum

_____ + _____ = _____
Pink   Red   Sum

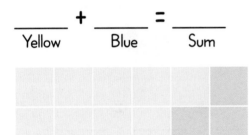

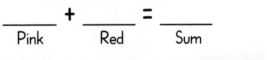

_____ + _____ = _____
Yellow   Blue   Sum

_____ + _____ = _____
Pink   Red   Sum

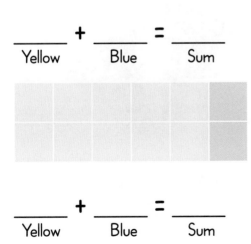

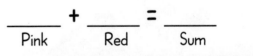

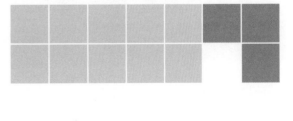

_____ + _____ = _____
Yellow   Blue   Sum

_____ + _____ = _____
Pink   Red   Sum

ACTIVITY 32 · DOUBLES

PEPPERONI PIES

Count how many pieces of pepperoni are on each slice of pizza. What do you notice about each plate? That's right! When you see two things with the same amount, it's called a **double**! Write the doubles that sum up the pepperoni pieces.

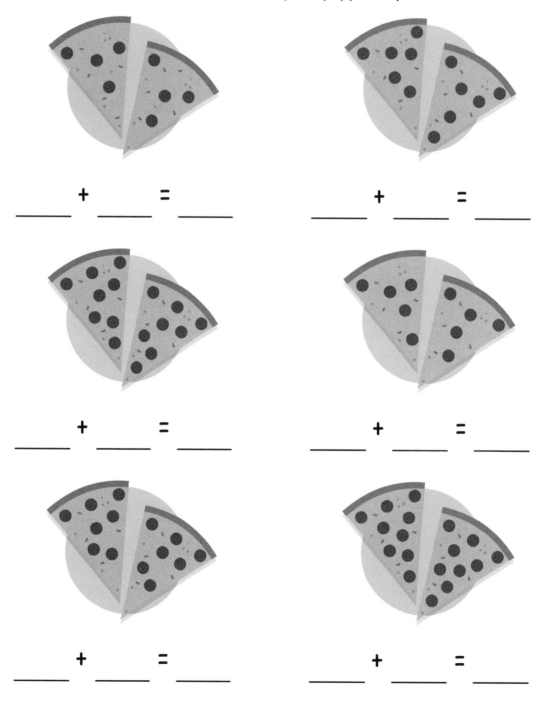

_____ + _____ = _____   _____ + _____ = _____

_____ + _____ = _____   _____ + _____ = _____

_____ + _____ = _____   _____ + _____ = _____

ACTIVITY 33 • SUM & DIFFERENCE

CARNIVAL CALCULATION

Jerry took his family to the carnival. Help him **calculate** how much of each item he had by the end of the day. Complete the number sentences. Then put the answers in the matching boxes at the bottom.

_____ + _____

_____ + _____

_____ + _____

_____ + _____

41

ACTIVITY 34 • REGROUPING

YOUR FRIEND 10

Making 10 is really important to help us count *BEYOND* 10. When you rearrange ten frames, you can think of making new numbers to add in your mind.

Let's think of this:

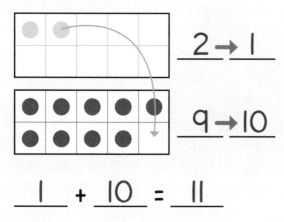

$2 \rightarrow 1$

$9 \rightarrow 10$

___1___ + ___10___ = ___11___

Here we see 2 + 9 = 11.

Can you imagine moving one of the yellow dots for the 2 to the spot after 9 blue dots? Now you are left with adding 1 + 10, which equals 11.

This idea is called **regrouping**—or making a new group of 10 to make it easier to **solve** the equation.

Now try regrouping these sets.

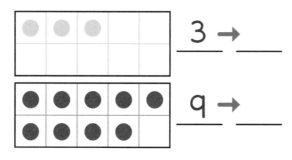

$3 \rightarrow$ ___

$9 \rightarrow$ ___

_____ + _____ = _____

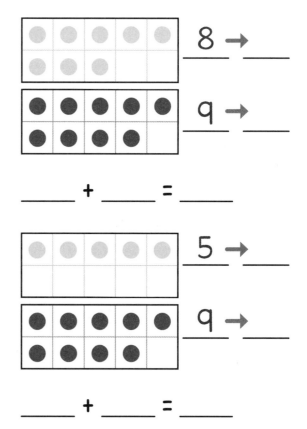

$8 \rightarrow$ ___

$9 \rightarrow$ ___

_____ + _____ = _____

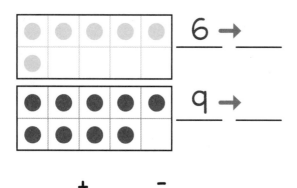

$6 \rightarrow$ ___

$9 \rightarrow$ ___

_____ + _____ = _____

$5 \rightarrow$ ___

$9 \rightarrow$ ___

_____ + _____ = _____

ACTIVITY 35 · REGROUPING

8 IS GREAT

On the last page you regrouped 9 to make a 10. Isn't 8 also close to 10? When you see 8 added to another number, you can also try regrouping! Let's practice.

Let's think of this:

Here, you move 2 dots down instead of 1. It's the same method, just a new number of dots. Fun!

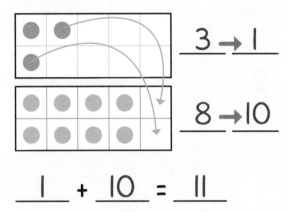

3 → 1

8 → 10

__1__ + __10__ = __11__

Now try regrouping these sets.

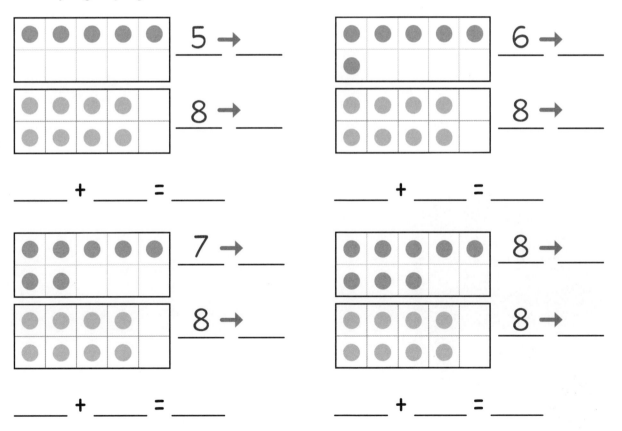

5 → ___

8 → ___

___ + ___ = ___

6 → ___

8 → ___

___ + ___ = ___

7 → ___

8 → ___

___ + ___ = ___

8 → ___

8 → ___

___ + ___ = ___

ADDING IT UP

ACTIVITY 36 • PROBLEM-SOLVING

KYLE'S GAMES

Kyle played three games on the weekend. After the first game,
he was sad because he didn't score any baskets. But he didn't give up!
By the end of all three games, he had scored 30 baskets.
How many baskets could he have scored in each of the last two games?
Explain your thinking to a grown-up. Answers will vary.

Game 1	Game 2	Game 3
0		

ACTIVITY 37 • NUMBER SENTENCES

DOGGY DANCE

Lilo is having a dog dance party! Help her count her dog friends in each group, then add them together in a number sentence.

[ ] + [ ] = [ ]   [ ] + [ ] = [ ]

[ ] + [ ] = [ ]   [ ] + [ ] = [ ]

ACTIVITY 38 · FACT FAMILIES

MORE PATTERNS

Count the number of blocks in each set. Then tell a grown-up a pattern you notice in the orange and purple blocks. What pattern do you see in the yellow and pink blocks? How about the green and red blocks?

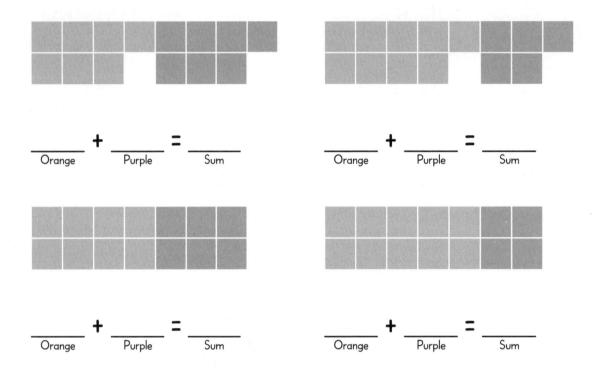

_____ + _____ = _____
Orange   Purple   Sum

_____ + _____ = _____
Orange   Purple   Sum

_____ + _____ = _____
Orange   Purple   Sum

_____ + _____ = _____
Orange   Purple   Sum

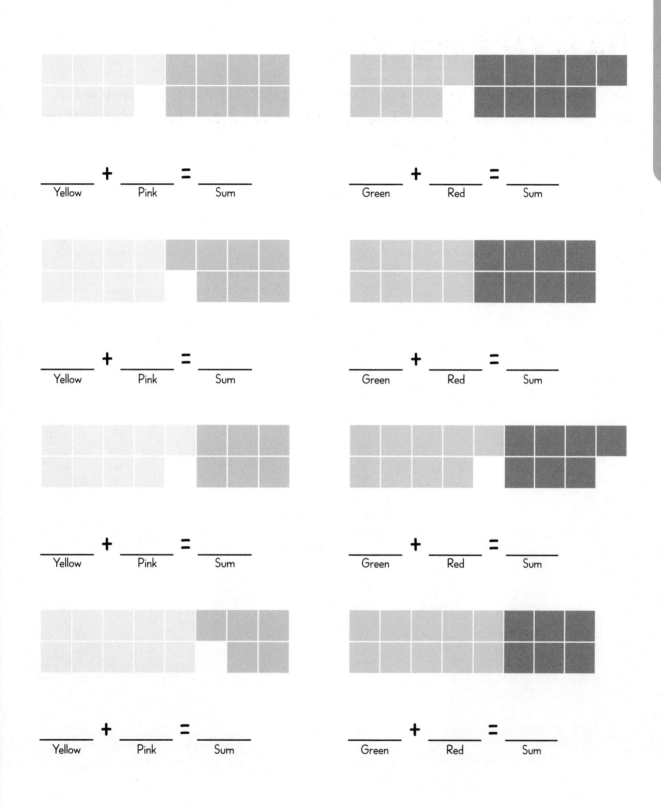

_____ + _____ = _____
Yellow   Pink   Sum

_____ + _____ = _____
Green   Red   Sum

_____ + _____ = _____
Yellow   Pink   Sum

_____ + _____ = _____
Green   Red   Sum

_____ + _____ = _____
Yellow   Pink   Sum

_____ + _____ = _____
Green   Red   Sum

_____ + _____ = _____
Yellow   Pink   Sum

_____ + _____ = _____
Green   Red   Sum

ACTIVITY 39 · NUMBER SENTENCES

DAILYN'S DOZENS

Dailyn wants to fill each carton of eggs. Circle different combinations and use them to write your own number sentences. Each equation will add up to 12 eggs. Answers will vary.

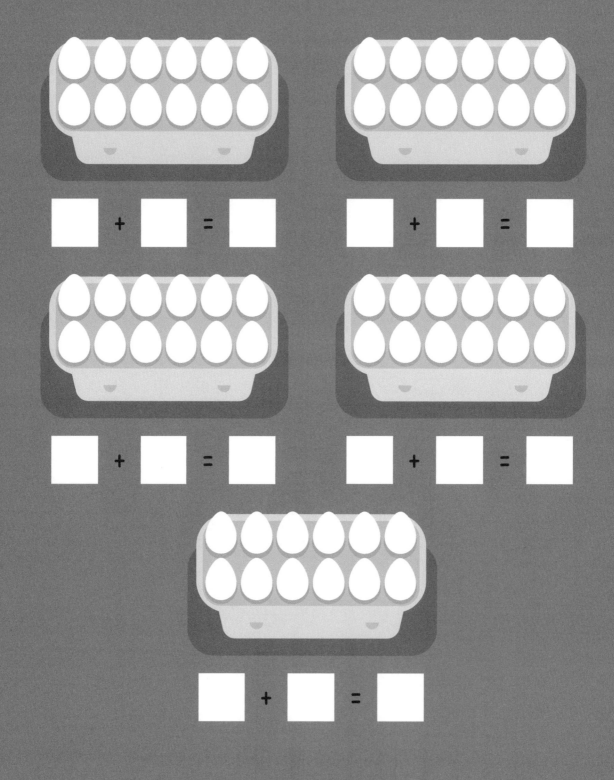

NICK'S NUMBER LINE

Nick uses a number line to show how he can add two numbers. Complete the equations.

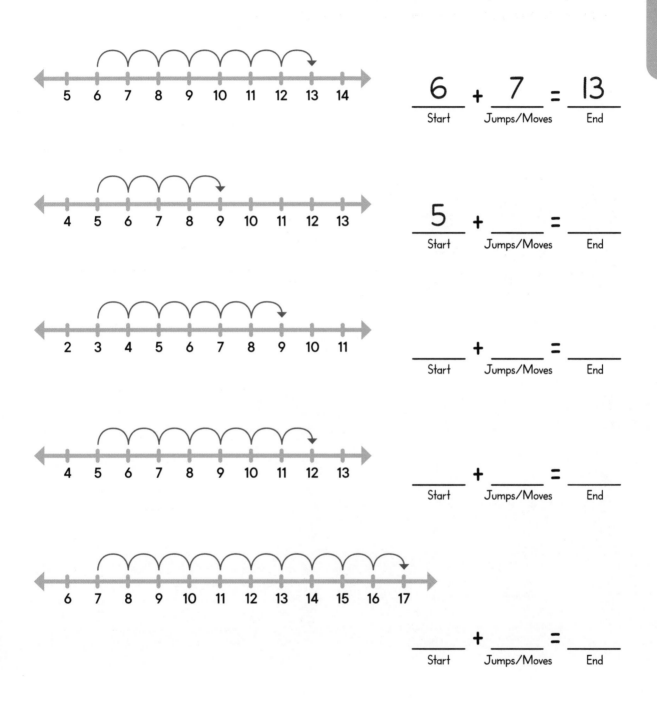

$$\underset{\text{Start}}{6} + \underset{\text{Jumps/Moves}}{7} = \underset{\text{End}}{13}$$

$$\underset{\text{Start}}{5} + \underset{\text{Jumps/Moves}}{\rule{2cm}{0.4pt}} = \underset{\text{End}}{\rule{2cm}{0.4pt}}$$

$$\underset{\text{Start}}{\rule{2cm}{0.4pt}} + \underset{\text{Jumps/Moves}}{\rule{2cm}{0.4pt}} = \underset{\text{End}}{\rule{2cm}{0.4pt}}$$

$$\underset{\text{Start}}{\rule{2cm}{0.4pt}} + \underset{\text{Jumps/Moves}}{\rule{2cm}{0.4pt}} = \underset{\text{End}}{\rule{2cm}{0.4pt}}$$

$$\underset{\text{Start}}{\rule{2cm}{0.4pt}} + \underset{\text{Jumps/Moves}}{\rule{2cm}{0.4pt}} = \underset{\text{End}}{\rule{2cm}{0.4pt}}$$

ACTIVITY 41 • NUMBER SENTENCES

DEVONTE'S DOUGHNUTS

Help Devonte make different **combinations** of doughnuts. Create equations based on the types of doughnuts you see. Answers will vary.

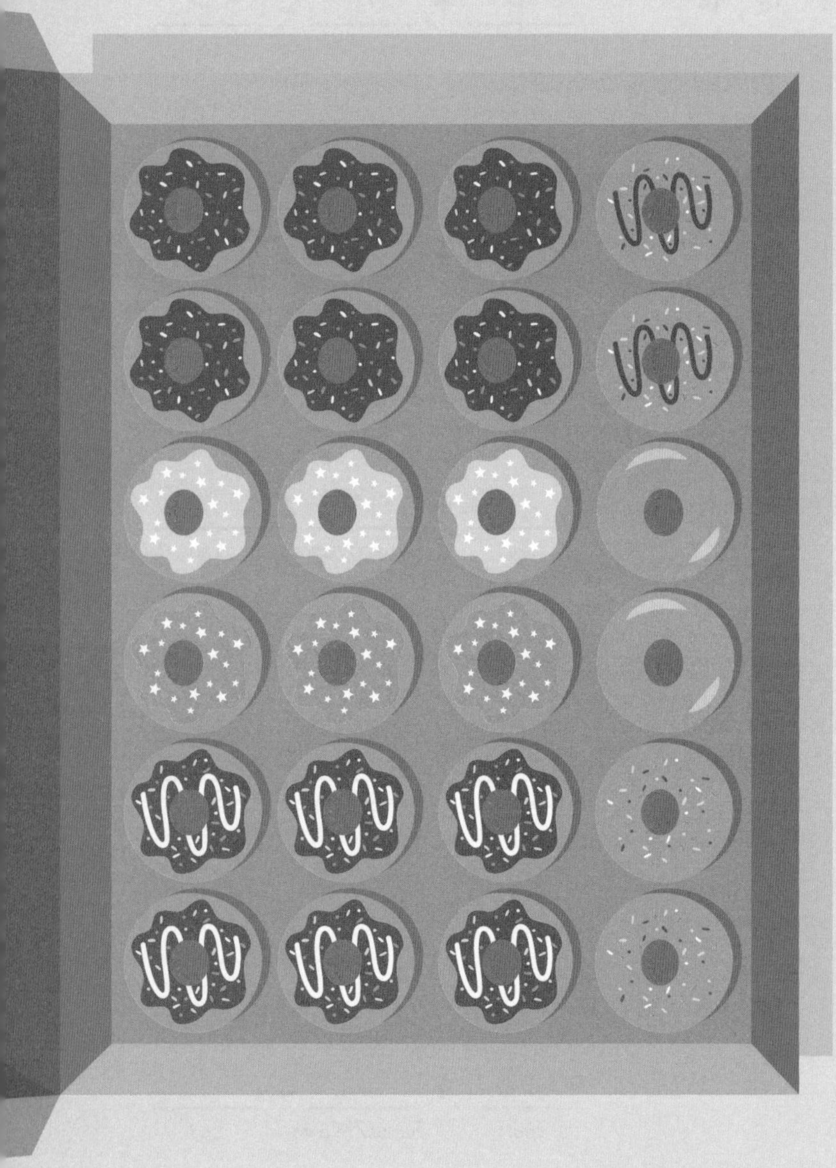

_____ + _____ = _____

_____ + _____ = _____

_____ + _____ = _____

_____ + _____ = _____

_____ + _____ = _____

ACTIVITY 42 • NUMBER SENTENCES

CARNIVAL COUNTS

You are allowed to spend 15 dollars ($) on two items at the carnival! Which pairs of items can you buy so that you spend all $15?

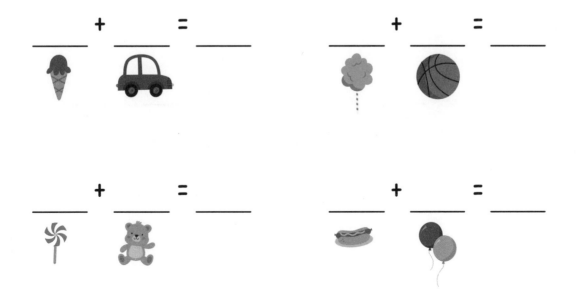

ACTIVITY 43 • FACT FAMILIES

EVEN MORE PATTERNS

Count the number of blocks in each set. Then tell a grown-up a pattern you notice in the green and yellow blocks. What pattern do you see in the blue and pink blocks? How about the orange and red blocks?

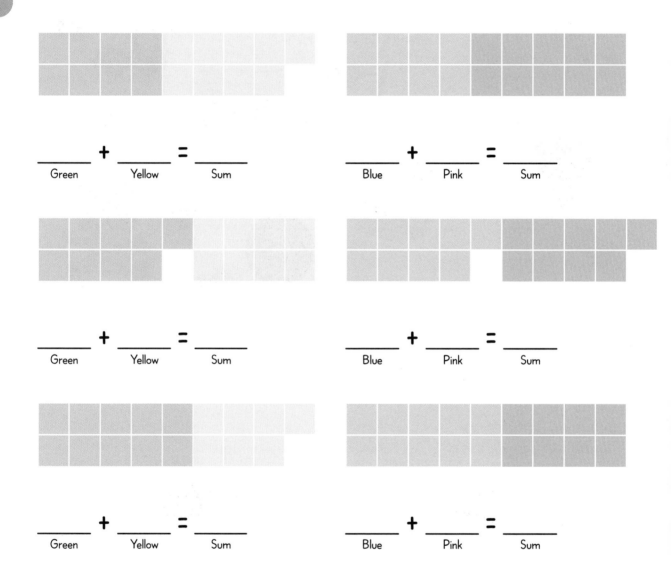

_____ + _____ = _____
Green   Yellow   Sum

_____ + _____ = _____
Blue   Pink   Sum

_____ + _____ = _____
Green   Yellow   Sum

_____ + _____ = _____
Blue   Pink   Sum

_____ + _____ = _____
Green   Yellow   Sum

_____ + _____ = _____
Blue   Pink   Sum

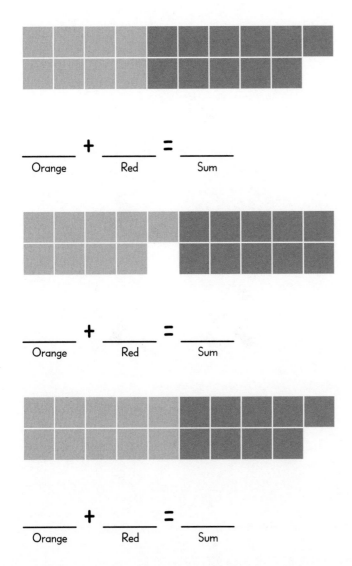

_____ + _____ = _____
Orange   Red   Sum

_____ + _____ = _____
Orange   Red   Sum

_____ + _____ = _____
Orange   Red   Sum

ACTIVITY 44 · NUMBER SENTENCES

BIRD BATH

For each fountain, choose two groups of birds, then write your addition equation.
Answers will vary.

_____ + _____ = _____   _____ + _____ = _____

_____ + _____ = _____   _____ + _____ = _____

_____ + _____ = _____   _____ + _____ = _____

ACTIVITY 45 · NUMBER SENTENCES

SPORT SORT

Choose combinations of balls and add them together! Answers will vary.

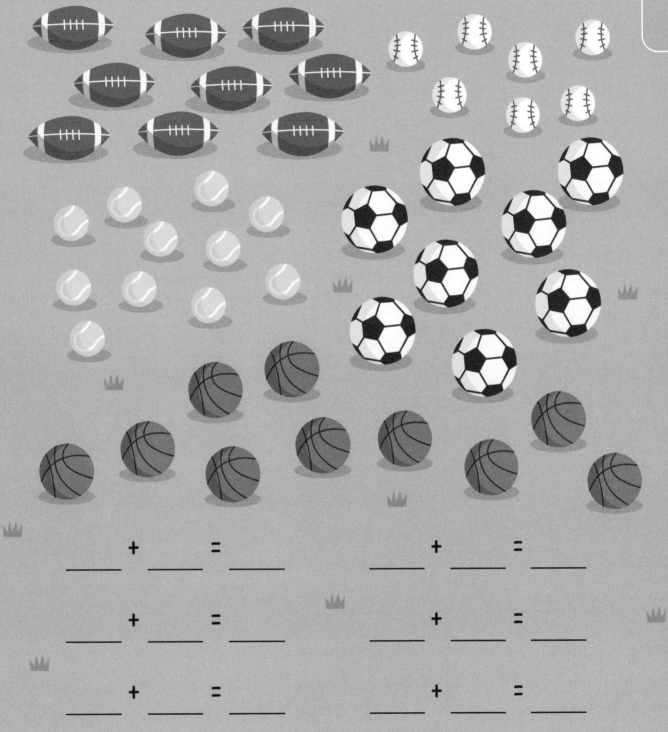

____ + ____ = ____   ____ + ____ = ____

____ + ____ = ____   ____ + ____ = ____

____ + ____ = ____   ____ + ____ = ____

Review/Practice

$1 + 1 =$ _____

$1 + 2 =$ _____

$2 + 2 =$ _____

$2 + 3 =$ _____

$3 + 3 =$ _____

$3 + 4 =$ _____

$4 + 4 =$ _____

$4 + 5 =$ _____

$5 + 5 =$ _____

$5 + 6 =$ _____

$6 + 6 =$ _____

$6 + 7 =$ _____

$7 + 7 =$ _____

$7 + 8 =$ _____

$8 + 8 =$ _____

$8 + 9 =$ _____

CHAPTER 3

SUBTRACTING IT DOWN

Now that you've practiced adding up, in this next section you will practice subtracting! **Subtraction** is the opposite of addition. So instead of combining numbers, you'll be taking numbers apart. Instead of counting up, you'll be counting down. It's okay to use your fingers or other objects to help you figure problems out.

ACTIVITY 46 • FIND THE DIFFERENCE

BYE-BYE, BIRDIES

When you count down by taking away from the total, you are finding the **difference**! Find the difference of each set of birds and write the number in the cloud.

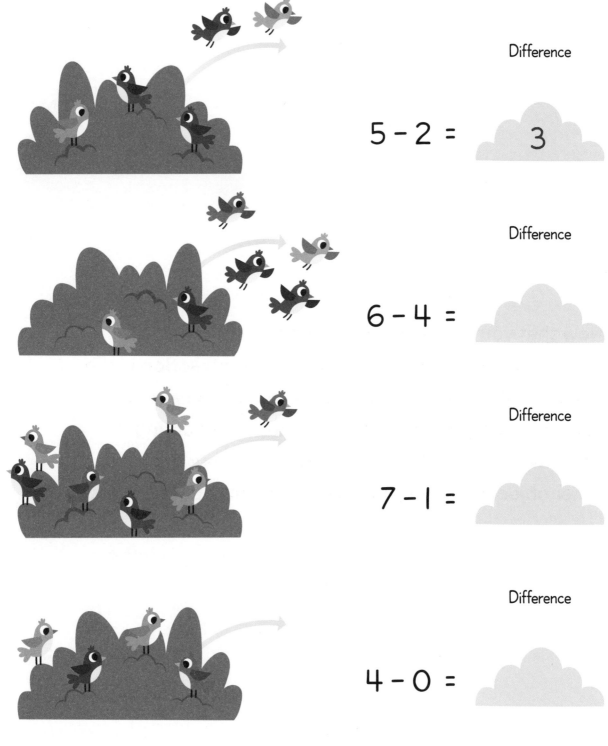

Difference

$5 - 2 =$ 3

Difference

$6 - 4 =$

Difference

$7 - 1 =$

Difference

$4 - 0 =$

58

ACTIVITY 47 · FIND THE DIFFERENCE
LISA'S PIZZA

Lisa ate some pizza slices. How many slices of pizza remain on each plate?

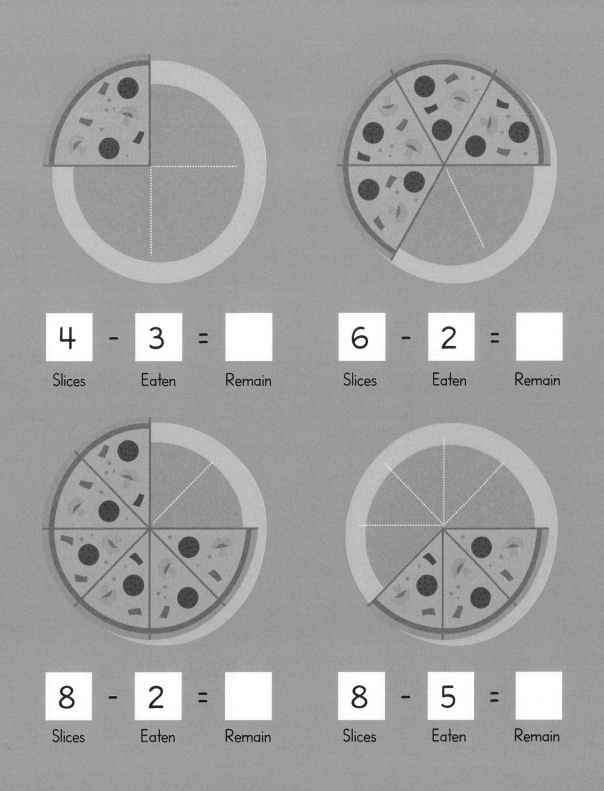

4	-	3	=			6	-	2	=	
Slices		Eaten		Remain		Slices		Eaten		Remain

8	-	2	=			8	-	5	=	
Slices		Eaten		Remain		Slices		Eaten		Remain

59

ACTIVITY 48 • FIND THE DIFFERENCE

TROY'S TREE TRIM

Troy trimmed some trees and leaves fell down. Complete the equation to show how many leaves remain on each tree.

$$\underline{10} - \underline{7} = \underline{}$$
Leaves   Fell   Remain

$$\underline{9} - \underline{6} = \underline{}$$
Leaves   Fell   Remain

$$\underline{7} - \underline{5} = \underline{}$$
Leaves   Fell   Remain

$$\underline{10} - \underline{4} = \underline{}$$
Leaves   Fell   Remain

ACTIVITY 49 • FIND THE DIFFERENCE
FLOWER PETALS

Nikki's garden has many beautiful flowers. Help her count how many petals remain on each flower.

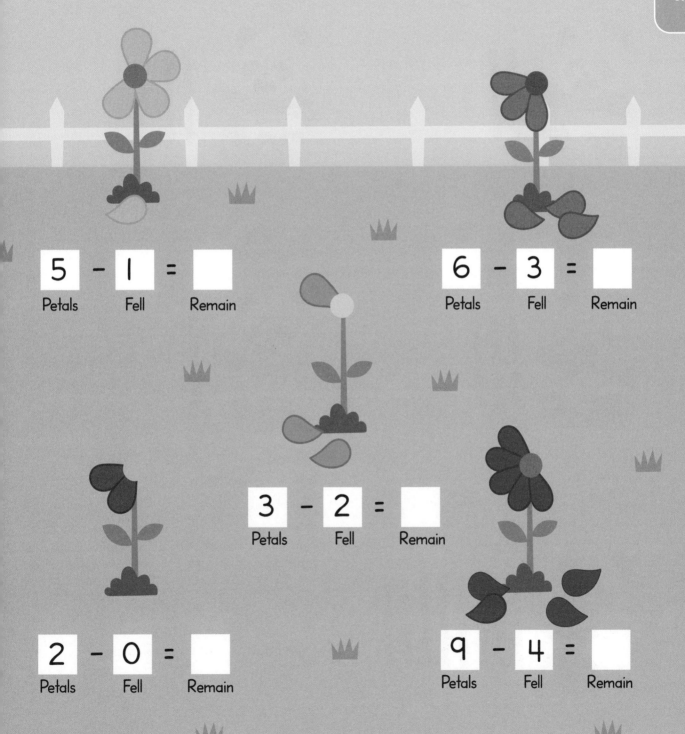

5 − 1 = ☐
Petals   Fell   Remain

6 − 3 = ☐
Petals   Fell   Remain

3 − 2 = ☐
Petals   Fell   Remain

2 − 0 = ☐
Petals   Fell   Remain

9 − 4 = ☐
Petals   Fell   Remain

ACTIVITY 50 • NUMBER SENTENCES

BAMBOO BITES

Po the Panda is eating bamboo. Write the number sentence for each set of bamboo Po eats and how many remain.

Bamboo   -   Ate   =   Remain

Bamboo   -   Ate   =   Remain

Bamboo   -   Ate   =   Remain

Bamboo   -   Ate   =   Remain

Bamboo   -   Ate   =   Remain

ACTIVITY 51 • NUMBER SENTENCES

LET'S TACO 'BOUT IT

Tanya's family eats tacos every weekday this week. Tanya eats some, then gives the rest to her sister. For each day, how many tacos does she have left to give to her sister?

★ **MONDAY** ★

☐ − ☐ = ☐

Tacos   Ate   For sister

★ **TUESDAY** ★

☐ − ☐ = ☐

Tacos   Ate   For sister

★ **WEDNESDAY** ★

☐ − ☐ = ☐

Tacos   Ate   For sister

★ **THURSDAY** ★

☐ − ☐ = ☐

Tacos   Ate   For sister

★ **FRIDAY** ★

☐ − ☐ = ☐

Tacos   Ate   For sister

ACTIVITY 52 • NUMBER SENTENCES

FRUIT BASKET

Evan grows fruit for the farmers' market. Count the total fruit in each section. Then write the number sentence that shows how many pieces of fruit Evan puts in the basket and how many remain.

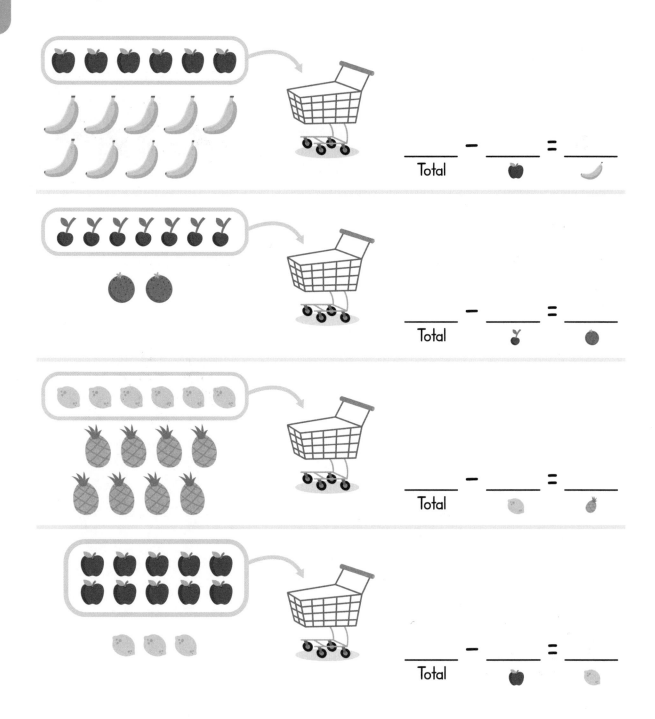

_____ – _____ = _____
Total

_____ – _____ = _____
Total

_____ – _____ = _____
Total

_____ – _____ = _____
Total

ACTIVITY 53 • NUMBER SENTENCES

MINUS THE METEORS

Wes the space ranger is blasting meteors. Write the number sentence for the amount he blasts and misses.

☐ – ☐ = ☐

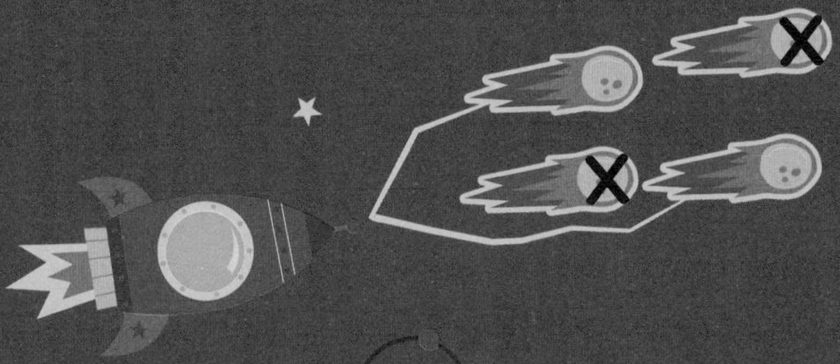

Meteors Blasted Missed

☐ – ☐ = ☐

Meteors Blasted Missed

☐ – ☐ = ☐

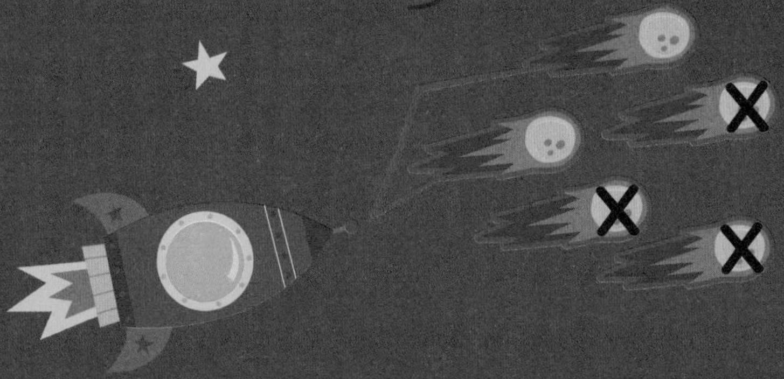

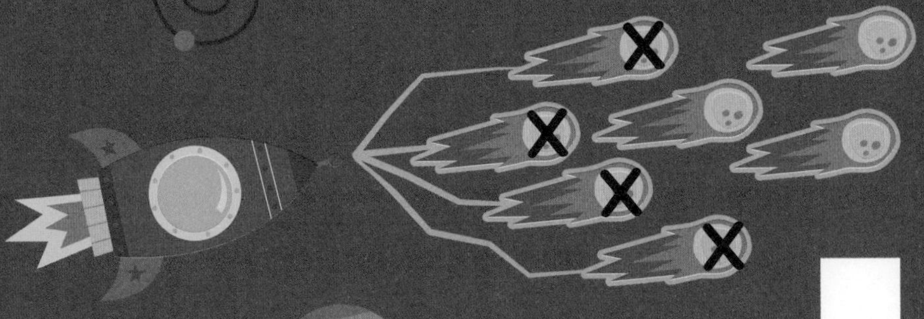

Meteors Blasted Missed

ACTIVITY 54 · NUMBER SENTENCES

HOW MANY MORE SHAPES?

For each set of shapes, write a number sentence to show the difference between the two shape types. For example, the difference between triangles and circles.

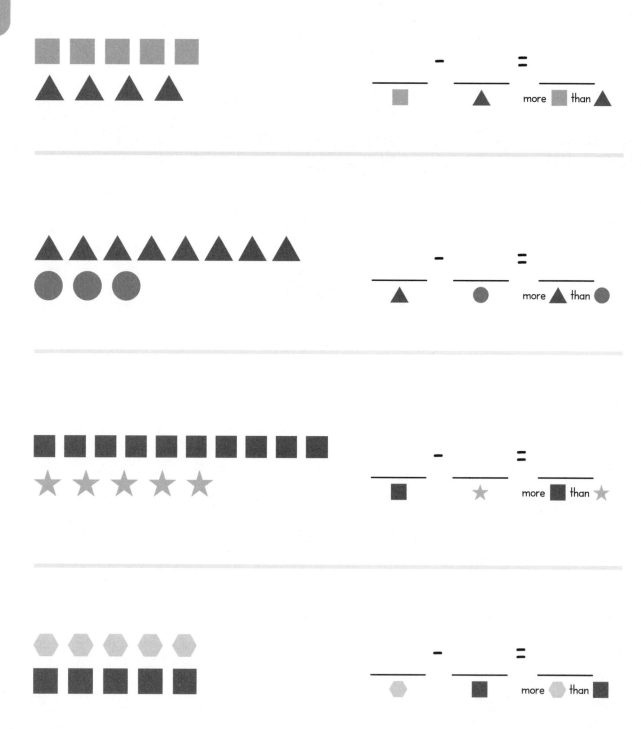

ACTIVITY 55 • NUMBER SENTENCES

VIOLET'S FARM

Violet wants to **compare** the counts of animals. For each set of animals, write a number sentence to show the difference between the counts of each.

☐ − ☐ = ☐
Horses Sheep Difference

☐ − ☐ = ☐
Chickens Pigs Difference

☐ − ☐ = ☐
Pigs Chickens Difference

☐ − ☐ = ☐
Sheep Cows Difference

67

ACTIVITY 56 • NUMBER SENTENCES

WARREN'S WEIGHT SCALE

Warren is weighing his toys. Help him find out how many more of each toy he has on the heavier side.

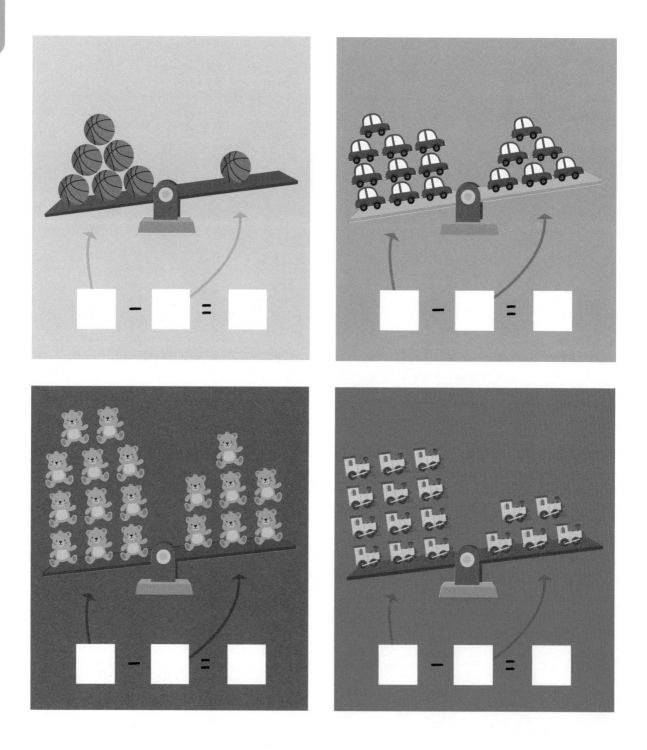

68

ACTIVITY 57 • NUMBER SENTENCES

HOW MANY MORE HOPS?

The frogs need more hops to reach the end of their hopping journey. Write the equation for each frog to show the difference it hopped.

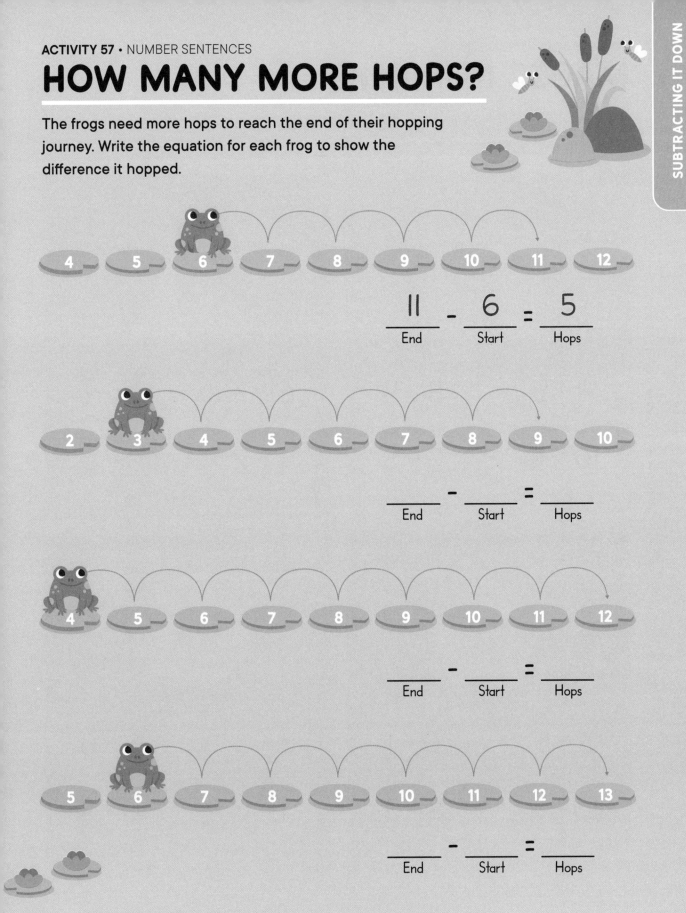

$$\underline{11} - \underline{6} = \underline{5}$$
End   Start   Hops

$$\underline{} - \underline{} = \underline{}$$
End   Start   Hops

$$\underline{} - \underline{} = \underline{}$$
End   Start   Hops

$$\underline{} - \underline{} = \underline{}$$
End   Start   Hops

ACTIVITY 58 · FACT FAMILIES

MAGIC NUMBERS

Circle all the number sentences that equal the magic number in the shape.

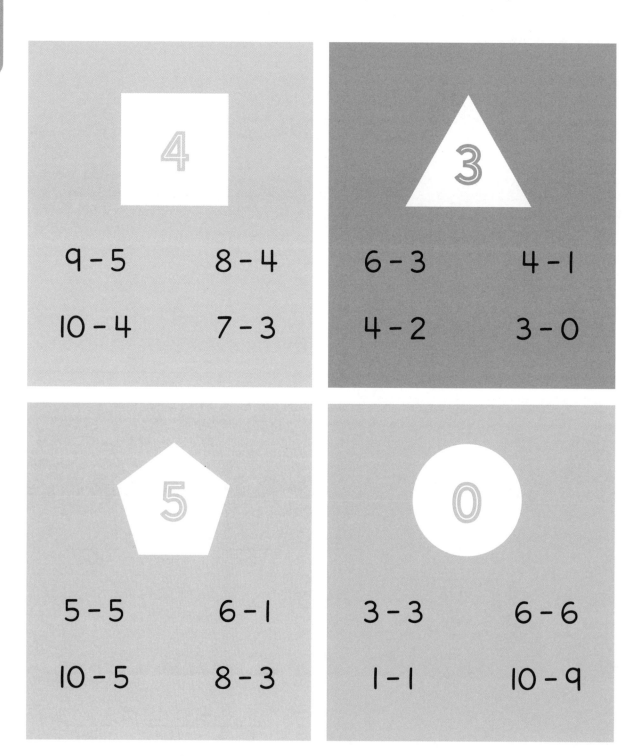

4

9 – 5   8 – 4

10 – 4   7 – 3

3

6 – 3   4 – 1

4 – 2   3 – 0

5

5 – 5   6 – 1

10 – 5   8 – 3

0

3 – 3   6 – 6

1 – 1   10 – 9

ACTIVITY 59 • FACT FAMILIES

MAGNET MINUSES

Match each equation to the correct difference in the middle. The magnetic differences in the middle can have more than one matching equation.

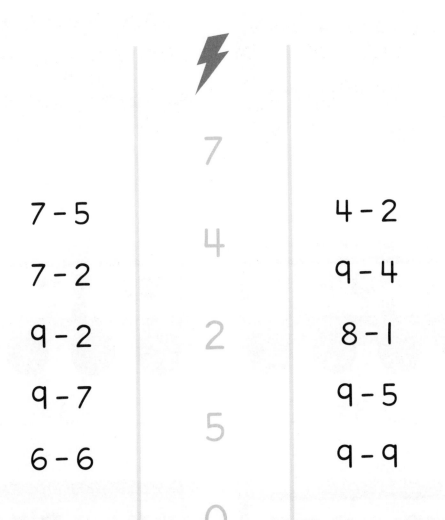

7 − 5   7   4 − 2

7 − 2   4   9 − 4

9 − 2   2   8 − 1

9 − 7   5   9 − 5

6 − 6   0   9 − 9

ACTIVITY 60 · FACT FAMILIES

HOW MANY  LEFT?

Josie is counting all the passengers in each train car. If 3 people get off from every train car at the next stop, how many passengers would she count in each train car? Write her equations.

_____ - 3 = _____   _____ - 3 = _____

_____ - 3 = _____   _____ - 3 = _____

_____ - 3 = _____   _____ - 3 = _____

ACTIVITY 61 • FACT FAMILIES

MORE MAGNET MINUSES

Match each equation to the correct difference in the middle.

The magnetic differences in the middle can have more than one matching equation.

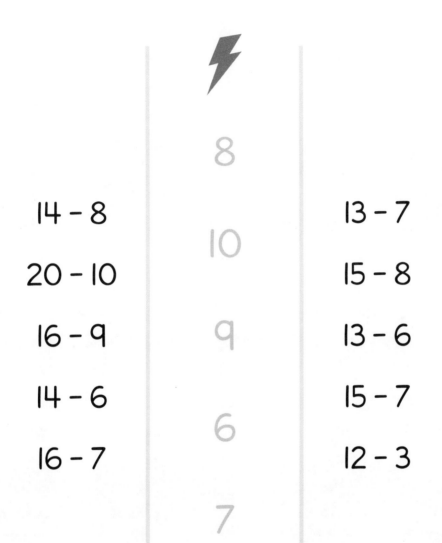

8

$14 - 8$

$13 - 7$

10

$20 - 10$

$15 - 8$

9

$16 - 9$

$13 - 6$

$14 - 6$

$15 - 7$

6

$16 - 7$

$12 - 3$

7

73

ACTIVITY 62 • FACT FAMILIES

BEYOND MY BOBA

Ryuto and Mikey like to compare who has more boba balls.
Help them compare the differences in boba balls inside their cups.

_____ - _____ = _____
Ryuto   Mikey   Boba

_____ - _____ = _____
Mikey   Ryuto   Boba

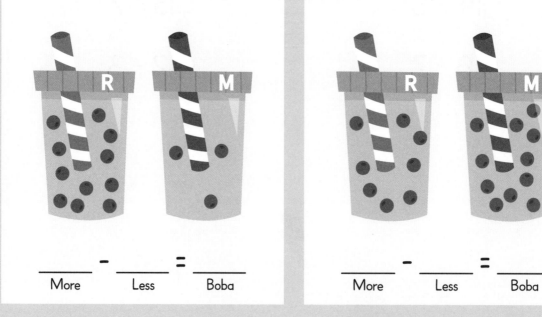

_____ - _____ = _____
More   Less   Boba

_____ - _____ = _____
More   Less   Boba

74

ACTIVITY 63 · DOUBLES FACTS

STRIKEOUT SUBTRACTION

Cross out the number of balls called by Emmett the umpire, then complete the subtraction equation.

10 – 5 = 5

75

ACTIVITY 64 · DOUBLES FACTS

HALF THE BOOKS

Knowing your doubles facts in addition is just as important in subtraction! Look at the double stacks of books and complete the fact family triangle and equation.

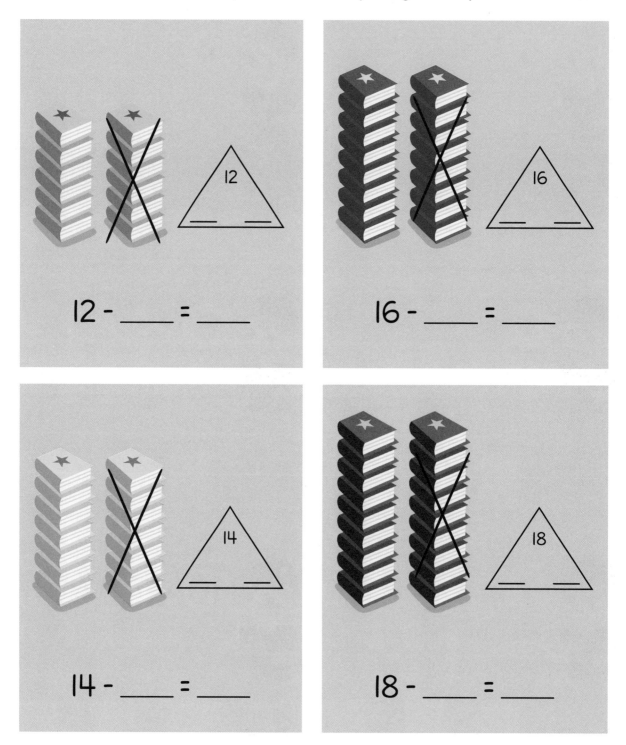

12 - ____ = ____

16 - ____ = ____

14 - ____ = ____

18 - ____ = ____

ACTIVITY 65 · FACT FAMILIES

WRITE THE FACT FAMILY

For each fact family, create subtraction equations that match the groups of shells.

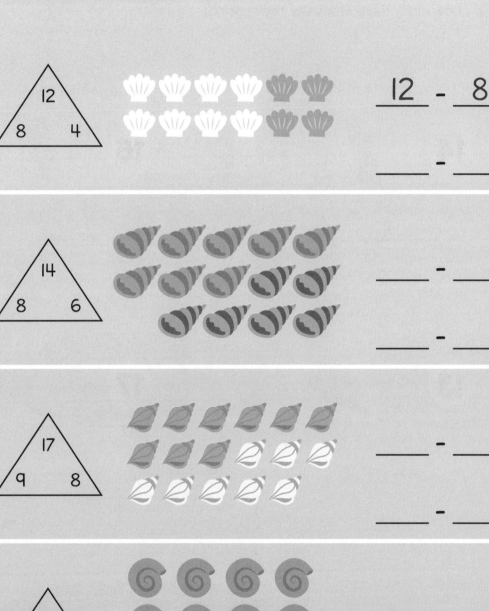

$12 - 8 = 4$

___ − ___ = ___

___ − ___ = ___

___ − ___ = ___

___ − ___ = ___

___ − ___ = ___

___ − ___ = ___

___ − ___ = ___

ACTIVITY 66 · REGROUPING

HANG 10

Emi likes to take at least 10 steps while she's riding her surfboard.
The numbers on the board show how many steps she took.
On the lines show how many more steps she took past 10.

14

10   4

16

____   ____

13

____   ____

17

____   ____

11

____   ____

18

____   ____

ACTIVITY 67 · REGROUPING

SUBTRACT FROM 10

When big numbers are tricky to subtract, try to break one of the numbers into friendly numbers like 10.

For 13 − 5, think of 13 as 10 and 3.
Then take 5 away from 10.
You're left with 5 and 3, which is 8!
So, 13 − 5 = 8.

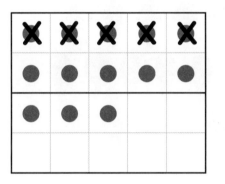

13 − 5 = _____

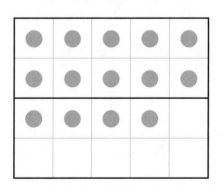

14 − 6 = _____

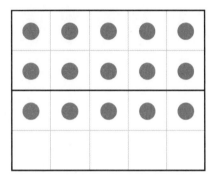

15 − 9 = _____

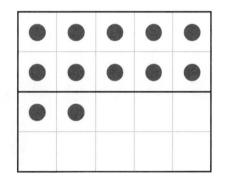

12 − 7 = _____

ACTIVITY 68 • NUMBER SENTENCES

COMPARING CONES

Ruby is comparing which ice cream flavors she sold today in her ice cream shop. First color in the squares that match the number of ice cream flavors she sold. Then help her find the differences between the flavors she sold.

15					
14					
13					
12					
11					
10					
9					
8					
7					
6					
5					
4					
3					
2					
1					

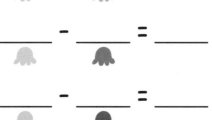

_____ - _____ = _____

_____ - _____ = _____

_____ - _____ = _____

_____ - _____ = _____

ACTIVITY 69 · NUMBER SENTENCES

AWESOME OLLIES

Wilder ollies (jumps) over the line of cones. Help Wilder complete the subtraction sentences to show how many cones he jumps and the number he lands on.

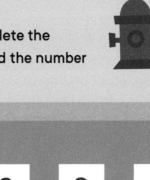

3	-	2	=	1
Starting #		Cones		Landing #

	-		=	
Starting #		Cones		Landing #

	-		=	
Starting #		Cones		Landing #

	-		=	
Starting #		Cones		Landing #

ACTIVITY 70 · COMPARING/NUMBER SENTENCES

DEREK'S DONATION

Solve the problems below and explain to a grown-up how you did it.

Derek had 15 toys he didn't need anymore. He donated 9 toys and gave the rest to his sister, Althea. How many toys did Althea get?

The 9 toys that Derek donated went to a new boy named Miles. Miles painted 6 of the toys. How many toys were not painted?

_____ - _____ = _____
Total toys   Donated   Althea's toys

_____ - _____ = _____
Donated   Painted   Not painted

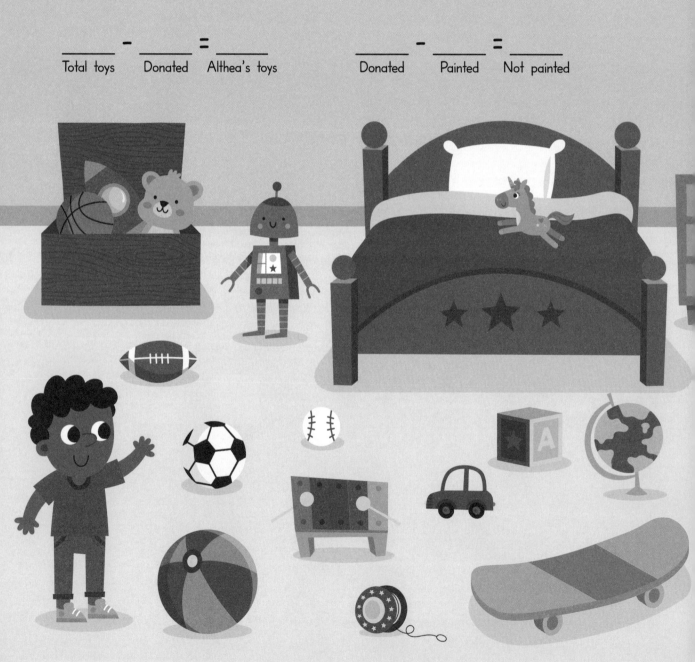

ACTIVITY 71 • NUMBER SENTENCES

SHOPPING TIME

Ryan bought some new items. Cross out the number of dollars he used for each item and complete the subtraction equation.

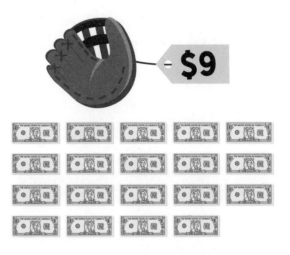

_____ - _____ = _____   _____ - _____ = _____

_____ - _____ = _____   _____ - _____ = _____

83

ACTIVITY 72 • COMPARING/NUMBER SENTENCES

FISHING FUN

Use the pictures to help you solve the problem. Explain your thinking to a grown-up.

Olivia and Zoey went fishing in a pond with 17 red fish and 14 purple fish. Olivia caught 8 red fish and Zoey caught 5 purple fish. Olivia said she left more fish in the pond. Zoey said they left the same amount. Who's right? Why?

Show your thinking here:

ACTIVITY 73 • NUMBER SENTENCES

FLY AWAY FEATHERS

Count the birds in each tree. Draw an X to cross out how many you want to fly away. Then make a subtraction equation. Answers will vary.

_____ - _____ = _____

_____ - _____ = _____

_____ - _____ = _____

_____ - _____ = _____

85

ACTIVITY 74 • NUMBER SENTENCES

BOWLING BUDDIES

Lindsey and Lani bowled three rounds. For each round, use subtraction to show how many pins they had left at the end of each round.

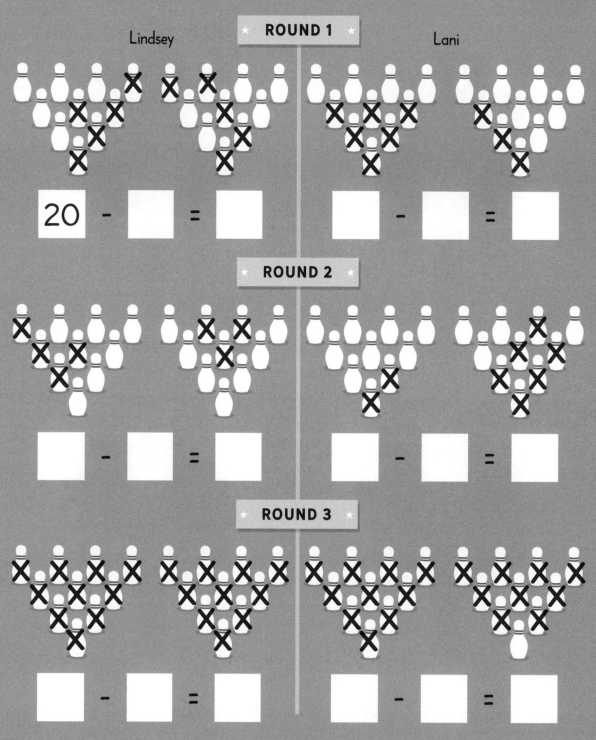

Lindsey ★ **ROUND 1** ★ Lani

20 - ⬜ = ⬜   ⬜ - ⬜ = ⬜

★ **ROUND 2** ★

⬜ - ⬜ = ⬜   ⬜ - ⬜ = ⬜

★ **ROUND 3** ★

⬜ - ⬜ = ⬜   ⬜ - ⬜ = ⬜

JORDAN'S JEANS

Jordan is hemming some of his big brother's old jeans so the legs are shorter. For each pair of jeans, find out the new sizes. Then put them in order from smallest to biggest, based on their final size after being hemmed.

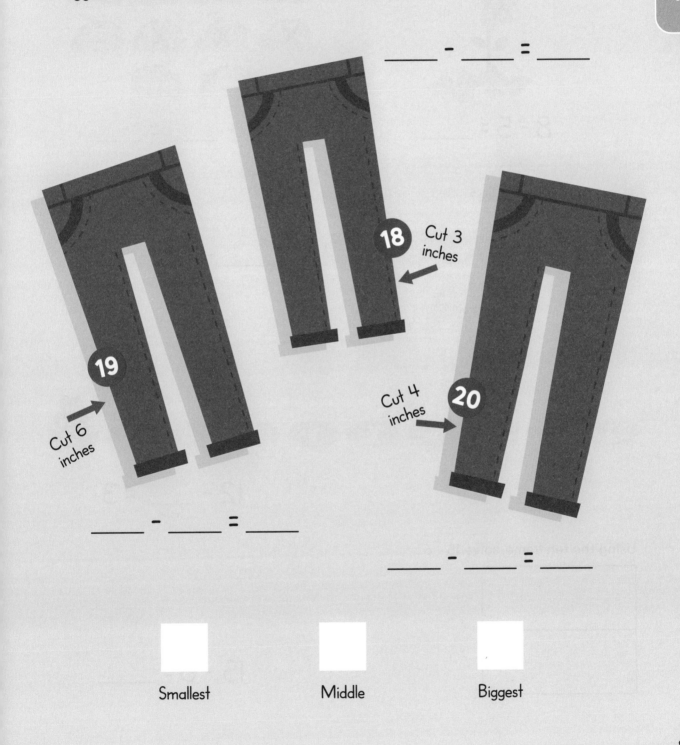

_____ - _____ = _____

18 Cut 3 inches

19 Cut 6 inches

_____ - _____ = _____

20 Cut 4 inches

_____ - _____ = _____

Smallest   Middle   Biggest

Review/Practice

Complete the number sentences.

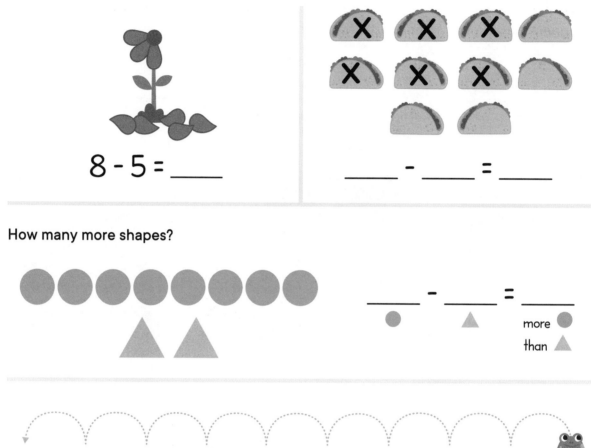

8 - 5 = _____

_____ - _____ = _____

How many more shapes?

_____ - _____ = _____

● more ●
than ▲

12 - _____ = 3
       hops

Using the ten frame, solve 15 – 6.

15 - 6 = _____

CHAPTER 4

UP AND DOWN WE GO

Be proud of yourself for doing an amazing job so far. Let's keep working hard! Here, you'll find a mixture of addition and subtraction problems, so pay close attention to which **operation** (+ or −) to use. There are also a few puzzles here, so put on your thinking cap and have some fun!

ACTIVITY 76 · IDENTIFYING THE OPERATION

FILL IN THE MATH SYMBOL

Help Keiri fill in the addition/plus (+) or subtraction/minus (–) symbol to show what's happening in each picture.

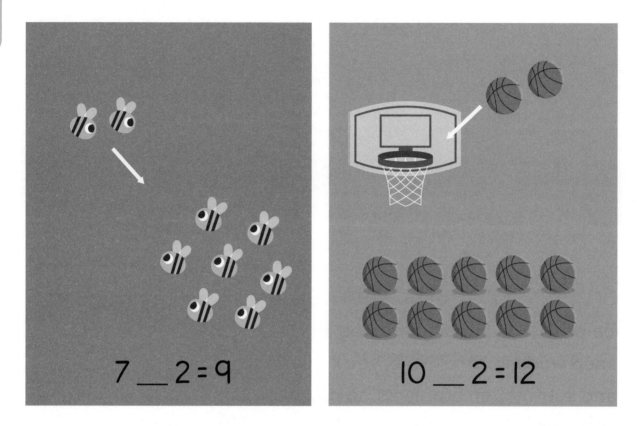

7 __ 2 = 9

10 __ 2 = 12

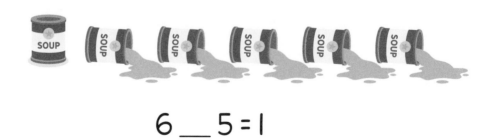

6 __ 5 = 1

ACTIVITY 77 • IDENTIFYING THE OPERATION

WHAT MATH IS HAPPENING?

Fill in the addition/plus (+) or subtraction/minus (−) symbol to show what's happening in each picture.

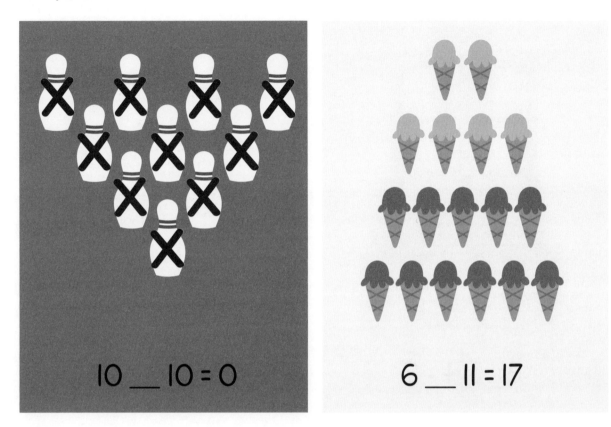

10 ___ 10 = 0

6 ___ 11 = 17

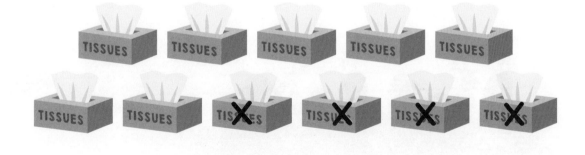

11 ___ 4 = 7

ACTIVITY 78 • IDENTIFYING THE OPERATION

WHAT'S THE MATH?

Fill in the addition/plus (+) or subtraction/minus (−) symbol to show what's happening in each picture.

6 __ 4 = 2

13 __ 4 = 9

11 __ 4 = 15

ACTIVITY 79 • IDENTIFYING THE OPERATION

WHAT'S THE MATH SYMBOL?

Fill in the addition/plus (+) or subtraction/minus (−) symbol to show what's happening in each picture.

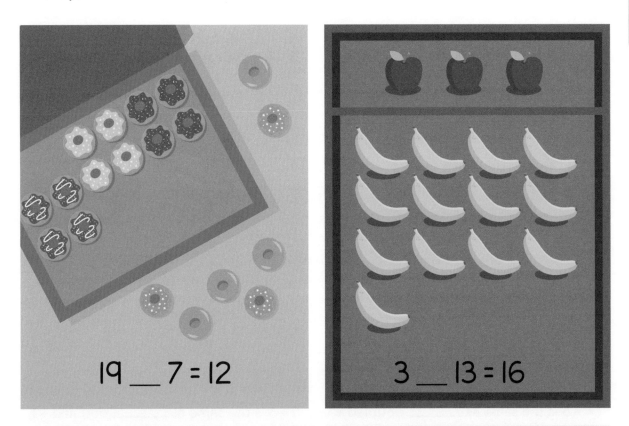

19 ___ 7 = 12

3 ___ 13 = 16

11 ___ 3 = 14

ACTIVITY 80 · DOUBLES + 1

FINDING DOUBLES + 1

Can you find the doubles? Circle the doubles and complete the sentences.

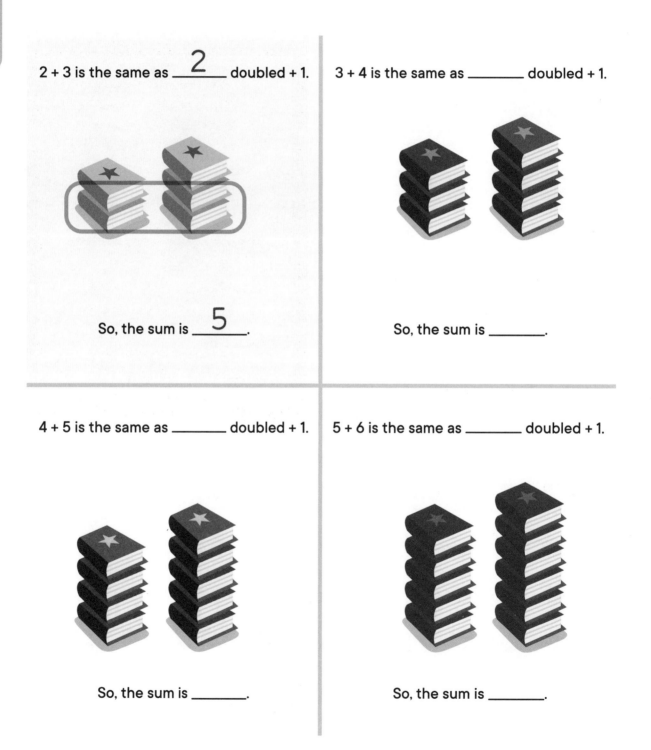

2 + 3 is the same as ___2___ doubled + 1.

So, the sum is ___5___.

3 + 4 is the same as _____ doubled + 1.

So, the sum is _____.

4 + 5 is the same as _____ doubled + 1.

So, the sum is _____.

5 + 6 is the same as _____ doubled + 1.

So, the sum is _____.

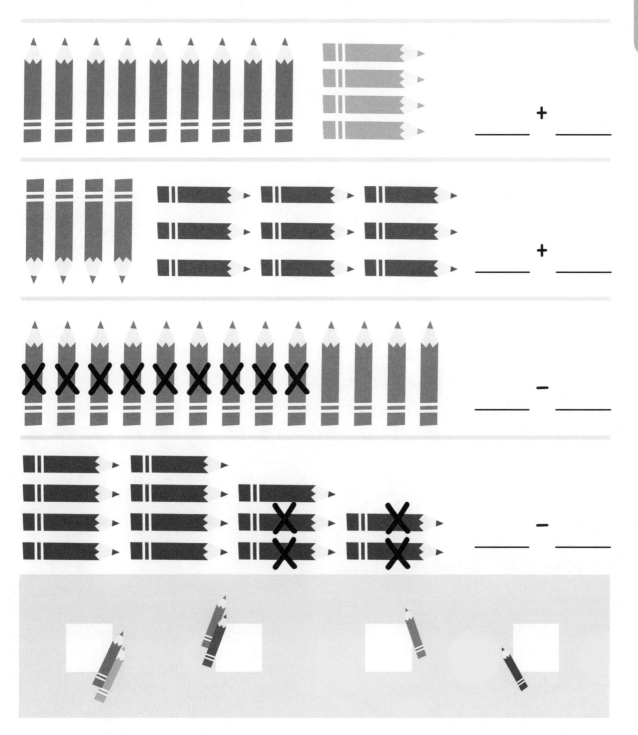

ACTIVITY 81 · SUM & DIFFERENCE

FREDDIE'S FACTS

Freddie remembered he can use fact families to help solve problems! Help Freddie find the solutions for each puzzle box.

_____ + _____

_____ + _____

_____ − _____

_____ − _____

ACTIVITY 82 · SUM & DIFFERENCE

CALCULATION STATION

Elliot's train needs special numbers to run. Solve each number sentence and put them in order from largest to smallest behind the train engine.

SHIP'S SHAPES

Help Captain Cayden calculate the different colors of each shape aboard his ship to reveal his treasure! Hint: Shapes with the same color can be different sizes, so use your clever pirate's eye!

____ + ____ =

____ - ____ =

____ + ____ =

____ + ____ =

ACTIVITY 84 • BREAK THE CODE

ALY'S ADVICE, PART 1

Aly was helping her sister, Ashley, who was having a hard time with math. Aly told Ashley some important words that really helped her. Solve the problems to see what she said.

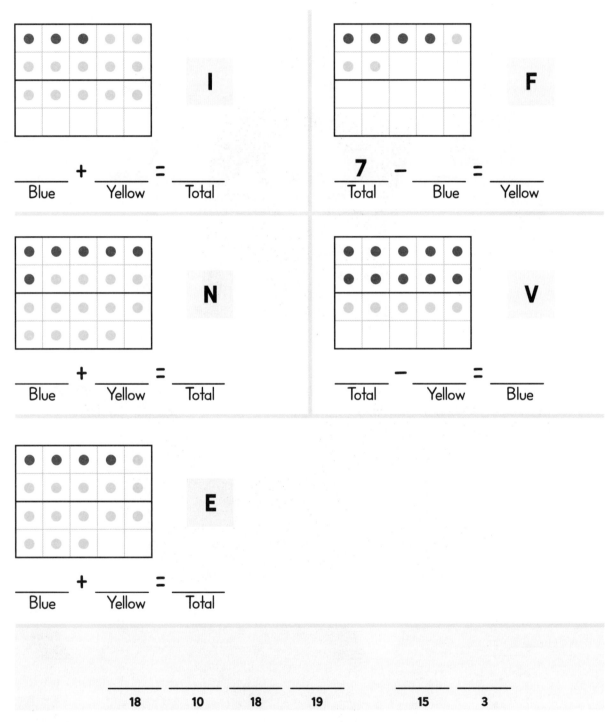

I

_____ + _____ = _____
Blue   Yellow   Total

F

7 − _____ = _____
Total   Blue   Yellow

N

_____ + _____ = _____
Blue   Yellow   Total

V

_____ − _____ = _____
Total   Yellow   Blue

E

_____ + _____ = _____
Blue   Yellow   Total

_____ _____ _____ _____   _____ _____
 18   10   18   19   15   3

Note to grown-ups: *There are four parts to this phrase, ending on page 101.*

ACTIVITY 85 · BREAK THE CODE

ALY'S ADVICE, PART 2

Solve the problems to continue seeing what Aly said to Ashley.

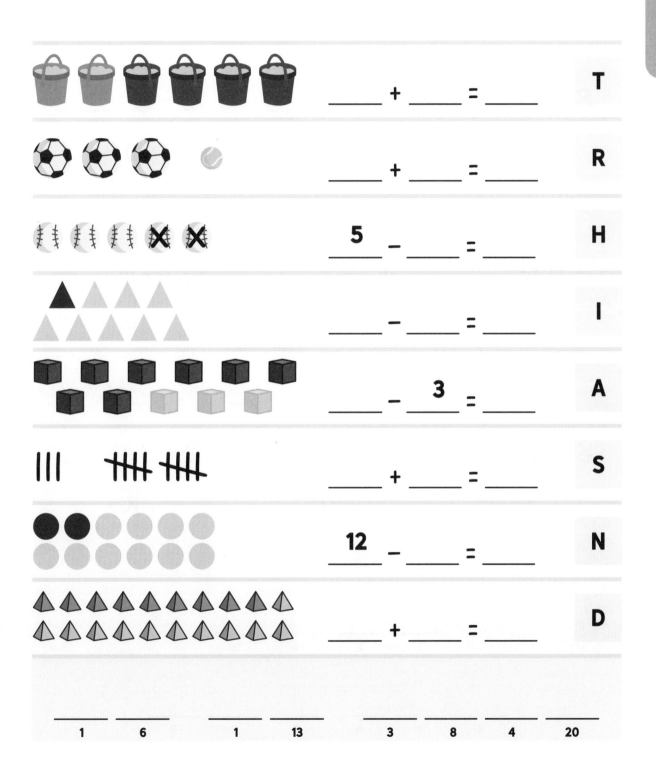

____ + ____ = ____   **T**

____ + ____ = ____   **R**

5 ____ − ____ = ____   **H**

____ − ____ = ____   **I**

____ − **3** ____ = ____   **A**

____ + ____ = ____   **S**

12 ____ − ____ = ____   **N**

____ + ____ = ____   **D**

____ ____ ____ ____ ____ ____ ____ ____
 1   6   1   13   3   8   4   20

ACTIVITY 86 • BREAK THE CODE

ALY'S ADVICE, PART 3

Solve the problems to continue seeing what Aly said to Ashley.

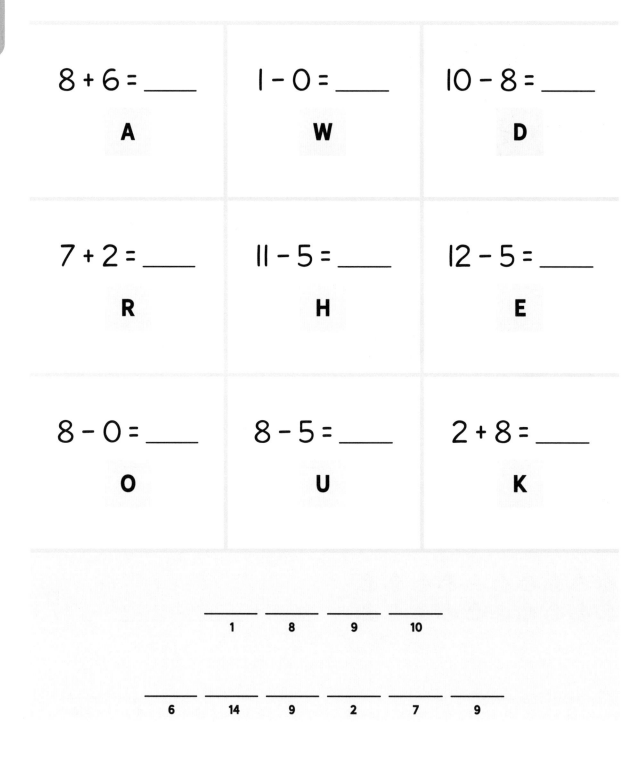

8 + 6 = ____

A

1 - 0 = ____

W

10 - 8 = ____

D

7 + 2 = ____

R

11 - 5 = ____

H

12 - 5 = ____

E

8 - 0 = ____

O

8 - 5 = ____

U

2 + 8 = ____

K

____ ____ ____ ____
1   8   9   10

____ ____ ____ ____ ____ ____
6   14   9   2   7   9

ALY'S ADVICE, PART 4

Solve the problems to finish seeing what Aly said to Ashley!

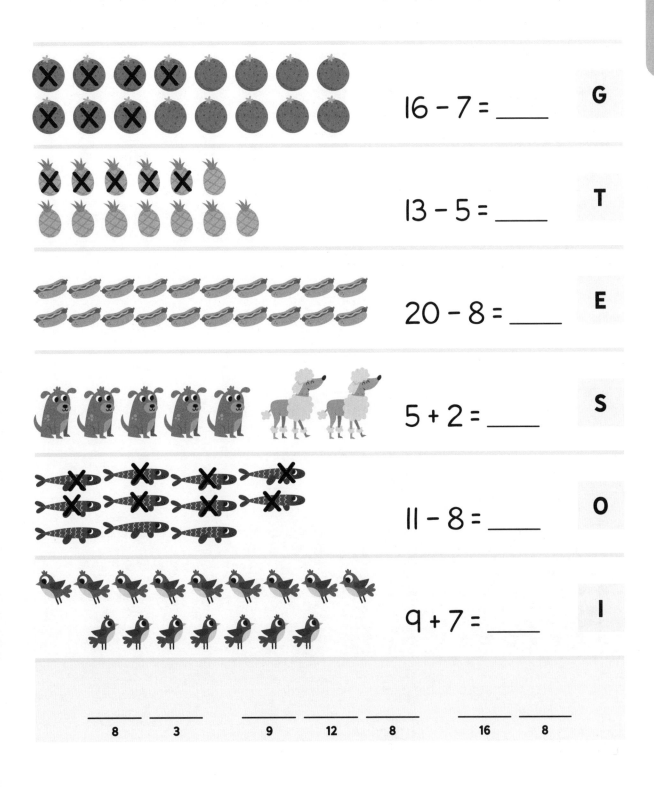

$16 - 7 =$ ___   **G**

$13 - 5 =$ ___   **T**

$20 - 8 =$ ___   **E**

$5 + 2 =$ ___   **S**

$11 - 8 =$ ___   **O**

$9 + 7 =$ ___   **I**

___ ___   ___ ___ ___   ___ ___
  8   3   9   12   8   16   8

ACTIVITY 88 • COMPARING

COACH CAM'S COMPARISON

Coach Cam is missing some sports balls. He wants to compare which number set of sports balls is **greater** after some balls were lost. Solve each equation and circle the item with the greater value.

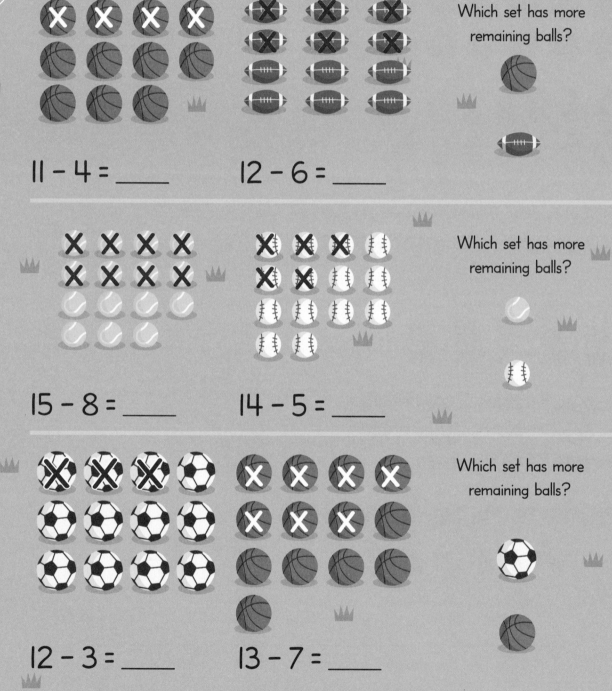

Which set has more remaining balls?

$11 - 4 =$ _____ $12 - 6 =$ _____

Which set has more remaining balls?

$15 - 8 =$ _____ $14 - 5 =$ _____

Which set has more remaining balls?

$12 - 3 =$ _____ $13 - 7 =$ _____

ACTIVITY 89 · COMPARING

BUFFET BALANCE

Lucas went to a lunch buffet and saw lots of food being eaten. He wanted to know which foods had more remaining. Solve and circle the item with the greater value.

$15 - 4 =$ ____

$17 - 5 =$ ____

Which number is greater?

$18 - 4 =$ ____

$18 - 7 =$ ____

Which number is greater?

$16 - 3 =$ ____

$19 - 5 =$ ____

Which number is greater?

COMPARING CARTONS

Eli bought the eggs labeled Carton A. Landon bought the eggs labeled Carton B. Solve the addition equations. Then circle which carton has **less** eggs in each set.

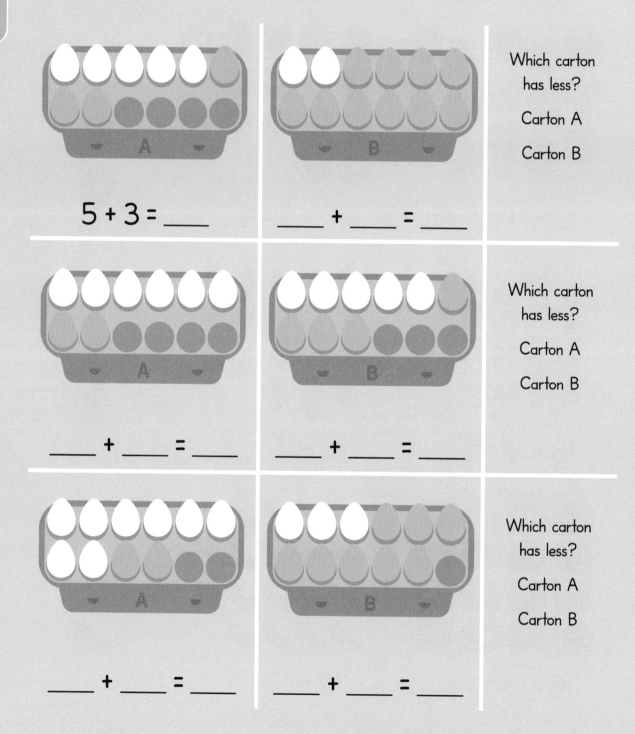

Which carton has less?

Carton A

Carton B

$5 + 3 =$ ____

____ + ____ = ____

Which carton has less?

Carton A

Carton B

____ + ____ = ____

____ + ____ = ____

Which carton has less?

Carton A

Carton B

____ + ____ = ____

____ + ____ = ____

ACTIVITY 91 · COMPARING

ALIENS AWAY

Space Captain Ava discovered alien ships from three planets!
But some ships flew away. Help her calculate how many of each
set were left. Then sort them in order from least to greatest.

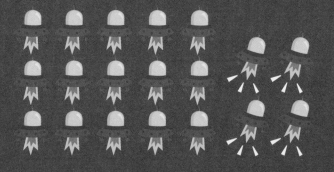

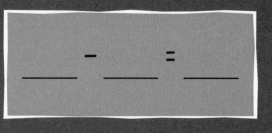

_____ - _____ = _____

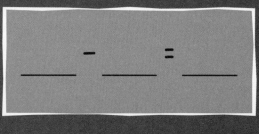

_____ - _____ = _____

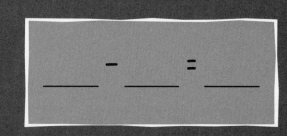

_____ - _____ = _____

Least ☐ ☐ ☐ Greatest

ACTIVITY 92 · NUMBER LINE

BUILDING BUDDIES

Four friends work in the same building and take the elevator up and down the floors. Number all the floors. Then use number sentences to show where they go.

If **Avery** goes down 5 floors,
what floor will she be on? _____th floor
Show a number sentence that can help you.

_____ − _____ = _____

If **Braxton** goes down 9 floors,
what floor will she be on? _____rd floor
Show a number sentence that can help you.

_____ − _____ = _____

If **Dahlia** goes up 5 floors,
what floor will she be on? _____th floor
Show a number sentence that can help you.

_____ + _____ = _____

If **Jasmine** goes up 9 floors,
what floor will she be on? _____th floor
Show a number sentence that can help you.

_____ + _____ = _____

Floor

Avery → 20 ___

___

___

___

___

___

___

Braxton → ___

___

___

10 ___

___

___

Dahlia and → ___
Jasmine

___

___

___

___

___

1 ___

ACTIVITY 93 • CREATE EQUATIONS

BROOKLYN'S BROOK

Brooklyn caught some fish. For each type of fish, cross out a group that she caught.
Then write a subtraction sentence for that group of fish. Answers will vary.

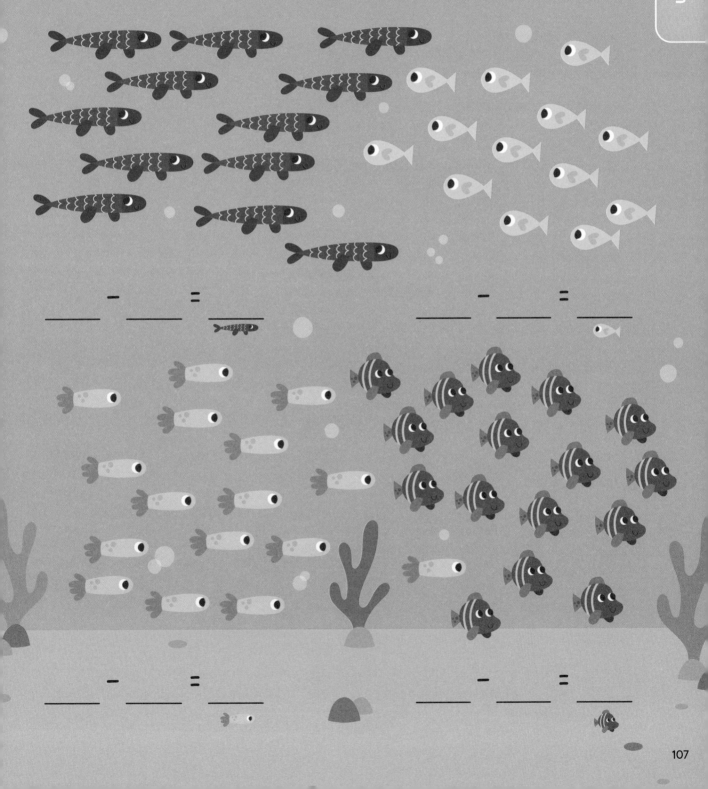

_____ − _____ = _____

_____ − _____ = _____

_____ − _____ = _____

_____ − _____ = _____

ACTIVITY 94 • CREATE EQUATIONS

ABBY'S ZOO

Abby the zookeeper is rounding up animals to put them to bed. Circle each set of animals. Write the total number of animals in each set. Then add the sets together so Abby can put the right number of animals to bed.

_____ + _____ = _____

_____ + _____ = _____

_____ + _____ = _____

ACTIVITY 95 · FACT FAMILIES

JONAH'S RACE CARS

Show 2 more cars that make 8.

Show 3 cars that make 12.

Show 3 cars that make 15.

ACTIVITY 96 · TRUE OR FALSE

TRUE OR FALSE?

Write T if the statement is true. Write F if it is false.

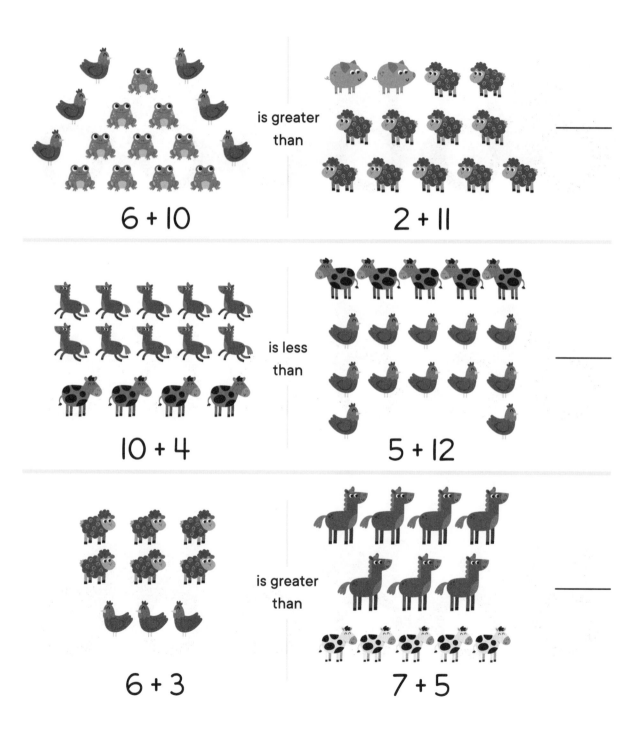

6 + 10   is greater than   2 + 11   _____

10 + 4   is less than   5 + 12   _____

6 + 3   is greater than   7 + 5   _____

ACTIVITY 97 • NUMBER SENTENCES/COMPARING

KAYLIE'S COSTS

Kaylie is shopping and wants to know which combination of clothes costs more or less. Help her calculate and circle the item or group of items that is less so that she can save money!

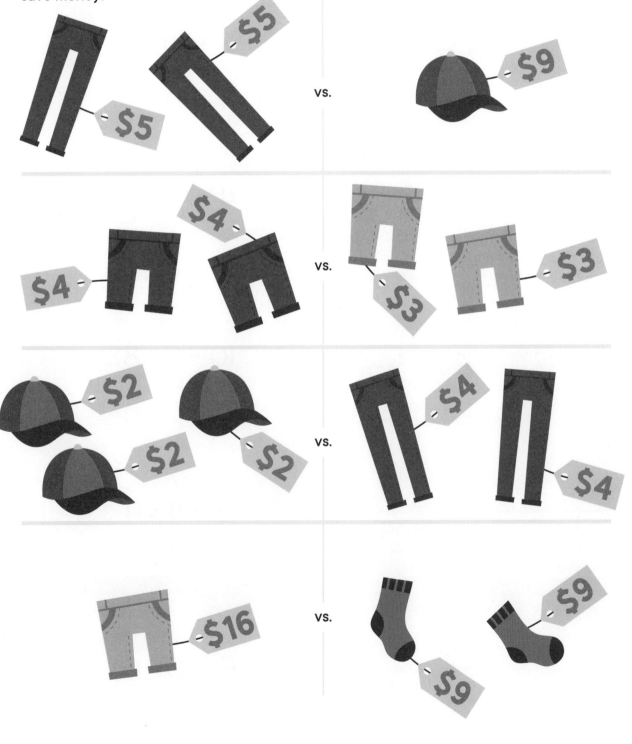

vs.

111

ACTIVITY 98 • TRUE OR FALSE

MARK'S MARKS

Mark marked some number lines and made equations. Circle T if the arrow on the number line matches the equation. Circle F if it does not match.

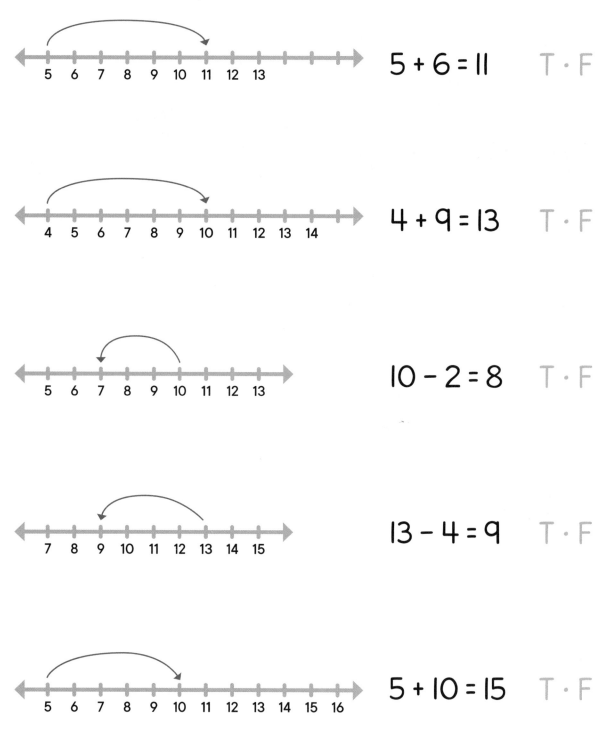

$5 + 6 = 11$ T · F

$4 + 9 = 13$ T · F

$10 - 2 = 8$ T · F

$13 - 4 = 9$ T · F

$5 + 10 = 15$ T · F

ACTIVITY 99 • STORY PROBLEMS
KEIRA'S PIE PROBLEM

Solve each problem below in a way that makes sense to you.
Explain to a grown-up how you thought about it.

Keira made 14 pies for her party. At the end of the party,
3 pies were left. How many pies got eaten?   _____

Keira couldn't eat the 3 pies that were left.
If she shared them with 4 friends, how much pie
could each friend get if they all get the same amount? _____

Note to grown-ups: *This second problem is known as an* **equal share problem**, *which touches on the idea of repeated subtraction. This concept leads to a greater understanding of division. In the practice of Cognitively Guided Instruction, we encourage teachers to try these types of equal share story problems with students as young as kindergarten. It's quite amazing to see what they come up with and their instinctive solutions and explanations. For example, "Each person gets a little bit less than one pie" is a very intuitive (and correct) answer!*

ACTIVITY 100 • STORY PROBLEMS

PEARL'S PIGGY BANK

Solve the problems in a way that makes sense to you.
Explain to a grown-up how you thought about it.

Pearl was saving her dimes to buy a gift for her dog.
On Friday she got 9 dimes for her chores.
On Saturday she got some dimes from the tooth fairy.
She counted 17 dimes in all.
How many dimes did she get from the tooth fairy?

_____

The next week, Pearl still had 17 dimes.
Pearl really wanted to buy some candy. It cost 4 dimes.
How much did she have left after she bought the candy?

_____

Review/Practice

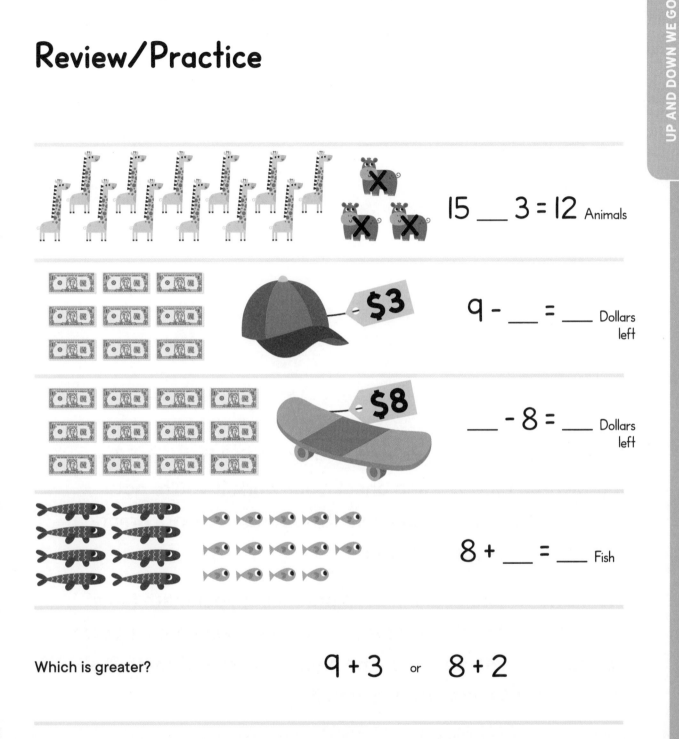

$15 \_\_ 3 = 12$ Animals

$9 - \_\_ = \_\_$ Dollars left

$\_\_ - 8 = \_\_$ Dollars left

$8 + \_\_ = \_\_$ Fish

Which is greater? $9 + 3$ or $8 + 2$

Which is less? $8 - 6$ or $9 - 4$

CHAPTER 5

THIS TIME IT'S TIMED!

Who's ready for some quick timed practice? If you are, have a grown-up time you and check your work. If you're not ready, that's okay. You can use this section as extra practice and try to time yourself later.

No matter where you are, keep practicing your math facts. Making mistakes is part of learning! Look over your mistakes to see if you can do better the next time around. Math is all about practice and sticking with it.

Note to grown-ups: *If your child expresses readiness to try the timed portion, set a timer for 3 to 4 minutes, depending on the section. If they express interest in going faster, try reducing the time by 30-second increments. You can find additional timed practice using this QR code:*

0-5 ADDITION

0 + 0 =	0 + 1 =	0 + 2 =
3 + 0 =	4 + 0 =	5 + 0 =
1 + 1 =	1 + 2 =	1 + 3 =
2 + 1 =	2 + 2 =	2 + 3 =
3 + 1 =	4 + 1 =	5 + 1 =
3 + 3 =	4 + 4 =	5 + 5 =
1 + 5 =	5 + 3 =	4 + 5 =
5 + 4 =	2 + 5 =	3 + 4 =
4 + 2 =	5 + 1 =	2 + 4 =
4 + 0 =	3 + 1 =	2 + 2 =
1 + 3 =	0 + 4 =	2 + 0 =
1 + 0 =	0 + 5 =	0 + 3 =
4 + 1 =	1 + 2 =	1 + 1 =
2 + 0 =	5 + 2 =	4 + 3 =
2 + 1 =	3 + 0 =	3 + 2 =

0-5 ADDITION

5 + 0 =	1 + 0 =	0 + 5 =
1 + 2 =	0 + 2 =	2 + 2 =
4 + 1 =	5 + 0 =	0 + 0 =
0 + 1 =	3 + 1 =	3 + 2 =
3 + 5 =	1 + 1 =	1 + 2 =
1 + 5 =	2 + 4 =	5 + 2 =
4 + 3 =	3 + 0 =	0 + 4 =
1 + 4 =	0 + 3 =	1 + 0 =
0 + 1 =	5 + 3 =	5 + 5 =
2 + 0 =	0 + 0 =	3 + 5 =
1 + 3 =	0 + 2 =	0 + 3 =
5 + 2 =	2 + 0 =	1 + 1 =
4 + 4 =	3 + 3 =	0 + 0 =
2 + 2 =	1 + 1 =	0 + 5 =
1 + 4 =	3 + 0 =	2 + 1 =

0-10 ADDITION

6 + 4 =	7 + 3 =	8 + 2 =
9 + 1 =	10 + 0 =	1 + 8 =
2 + 7 =	3 + 6 =	0 + 8 =
6 + 1 =	7 + 0 =	6 + 0 =
3 + 10 =	1 + 10 =	4 + 10 =
6 + 3 =	2 + 6 =	10 + 2 =
9 + 0 =	6 + 8 =	8 + 4 =
4 + 9 =	7 + 4 =	7 + 2 =
8 + 0 =	0 + 7 =	6 + 0 =
0 + 9 =	0 + 6 =	7 + 5 =
8 + 5 =	8 + 3 =	9 + 3 =
8 + 1 =	7 + 1 =	9 + 4 =
7 + 6 =	5 + 8 =	10 + 3 =
10 + 1 =	10 + 2 =	4 + 6 =
4 + 8 =	9 + 2 =	8 + 3 =

0-10 ADDITION

10 + 1 =	9 + 2 =	8 + 3 =
3 + 7 =	4 + 6 =	6 + 4 =
5 + 5 =	0 + 6 =	7 + 1 =
9 + 5 =	10 + 6 =	8 + 6 =
9 + 6 =	6 + 2 =	7 + 5 =
6 + 5 =	1 + 9 =	2 + 8 =
8 + 5 =	5 + 7 =	6 + 10 =
10 + 4 =	0 + 10 =	1 + 10 =
3 + 9 =	4 + 7 =	9 + 7 =
8 + 1 =	8 + 0 =	7 + 9 =
2 + 9 =	0 + 8 =	8 + 9 =
9 + 4 =	7 + 6 =	6 + 2 =
8 + 6 =	9 + 5 =	3 + 8 =
4 + 7 =	7 + 0 =	10 + 7 =
10 + 8 =	6 + 9 =	5 + 8 =

0-10 SUBTRACTION

0 – 0 =	2 – 1 =	3 – 1 =
3 – 1 =	5 – 1 =	4 – 0 =
5 – 2 =	4 – 4 =	5 – 4 =
5 – 0 =	6 – 5 =	7 – 2 =
8 – 7 =	8 – 1 =	7 – 1 =
7 – 7 =	8 – 8 =	7 – 6 =
9 – 9 =	10 – 10 =	9 – 6 =
8 – 6 =	6 – 0 =	7 – 0 =
0 – 0 =	2 – 0 =	2 – 2 =
7 – 3 =	6 – 2 =	5 – 1 =
3 – 0 =	4 – 1 =	6 – 3 =
5 – 4 =	6 – 5 =	9 – 5 =
7 – 3 =	8 – 7 =	8 – 3 =
9 – 3 =	10 – 4 =	11 – 5 =
10 – 6 =	10 – 9 =	6 – 4 =

0-10 SUBTRACTION

10 − 5 =	9 − 4 =	8 − 3 =
8 − 6 =	9 − 8 =	9 − 7 =
4 − 3 =	5 − 4 =	1 − 1 =
1 − 0 =	6 − 0 =	3 − 3 =
7 − 5 =	6 − 1 =	7 − 6 =
7 − 7 =	8 − 8 =	9 − 9 =
9 − 5 =	8 − 4 =	8 − 3 =
5 − 2 =	6 − 4 =	2 − 1 =
3 − 2 =	10 − 6 =	4 − 1 =
10 − 4 =	13 − 8 =	7 − 6 =
8 − 7 =	9 − 4 =	6 − 2 =
4 − 4 =	10 − 8 =	10 − 9 =
10 − 7 =	9 − 6 =	12 − 9 =
6 − 2 =	5 − 5 =	3 − 3 =
5 − 3 =	7 − 5 =	7 − 4 =

0-20 SUBTRACTION

7 – 0 =	8 – 0 =	9 – 0 =
10 – 0 =	9 – 1 =	10 – 1 =
11 – 3 =	11 – 2 =	11 – 1 =
15 – 5 =	15 – 6 =	15 – 7 =
13 – 8 =	12 – 7 =	11 – 6 =
9 – 1 =	12 – 4 =	15 – 7 =
17 – 9 =	18 – 9 =	19 – 9 =
14 – 8 =	13 – 7 =	12 – 6 =
12 – 8 =	12 – 5 =	14 – 7 =
14 – 9 =	10 – 2 =	10 – 4 =
8 – 2 =	9 – 3 =	10 – 4 =
13 – 5 =	10 – 1 =	9 – 0 =
10 – 0 =	13 – 4 =	13 – 6 =
16 – 7 =	16 – 9 =	11 – 5 =
15 – 5 =	20 – 10 =	15 – 9 =

0-20 SUBTRACTION

10 – 3 =	9 – 2 =	8 – 1 =
10 – 2 =	9 – 1 =	8 – 0 =
13 – 3 =	12 – 2 =	11 – 1 =
13 – 9 =	12 – 8 =	11 – 7 =
15 – 9 =	14 – 9 =	13 – 6 =
14 – 5 =	13 – 5 =	12 – 5 =
13 – 4 =	12 – 4 =	11 – 4 =
20 – 10 =	18 – 9 =	16 – 8 =
14 – 7 =	12 – 6 =	10 – 5 =
17 – 9 =	16 – 9 =	15 – 9 =
17 – 8 =	16 – 8 =	15 – 8 =
15 – 6 =	15 – 7 =	15 – 8 =
12 – 3 =	11 – 3 =	10 – 3 =
12 – 2 =	11 – 2 =	13 – 7 =
13 – 3 =	12 – 3 =	7 – 1 =

0-20 ADDITION & SUBTRACTION

12 − 7 =	12 − 8 =	9 + 9 =
8 − 4 =	6 + 4 =	11 − 4 =
10 − 8 =	8 + 4 =	6 + 6 =
11 − 9 =	11 − 6 =	9 − 7 =
9 + 7 =	9 − 4 =	8 − 5 =
10 − 2 =	7 + 6 =	11 − 8 =
8 + 7 =	12 − 6 =	6 + 8 =
20 − 5 =	6 + 5 =	2 + 3 =
5 + 9 =	11 − 2 =	7 + 5 =
2 + 6 =	9 + 3 =	12 − 9 =
12 − 8 =	9 − 5 =	9 + 5 =
4 + 8 =	11 − 9 =	9 + 4 =
5 − 2 =	8 + 3 =	10 − 6 =
8 + 8 =	12 − 7 =	2 + 8 =
9 − 6 =	9 + 8 =	7 − 2 =

0-20 ADDITION & SUBTRACTION

3 MINUTES

6 + 5 =	11 − 6 =	11 − 3 =
7 − 2 =	9 + 3 =	5 + 9 =
7 + 6 =	10 − 3 =	20 − 10 =
12 − 6 =	9 + 8 =	11 − 9 =
9 + 5 =	6 + 8 =	8 + 7 =
2 + 8 =	12 − 8 =	9 − 5 =
11 − 8 =	9 − 7 =	6 + 4 =
7 + 5 =	5 − 2 =	12 − 9 =
11 − 4 =	9 + 9 =	10 − 8 =
2 + 3 =	12 − 7 =	14 − 6 =
8 − 5 =	12 − 6 =	8 + 4 =
10 − 6 =	9 − 4 =	11 − 8 =
11 − 2 =	9 + 7 =	9 − 6 =
9 + 4 =	8 + 3 =	2 + 6 =
6 + 6 =	6 − 5 =	8 + 8 =

GLOSSARY

Note for grown-ups: These definitions are meant to support the language used in this book for your kindergartner.

add/addition: Combining two numbers to make a bigger number

addend: A number you add to another number

amount: A count of something

calculate: To figure out an answer using addition or subtraction

combination: Putting together two things

compare: Finding what is the same and different about two things

difference: The amount left after you take away some from another number

double: Two numbers that are the same

equal share problem: A problem where the total amount is shared equally between a number of groups

equation: A math sentence that uses symbols of addition (+) or subtraction (−) and equals (=)

fact family: Numbers that make equations that are connected when adding and subtracting. The numbers 3, 5, and 8 are in a fact family because $3 + 5 = 8$, $5 + 3 = 8$, $8 − 5 = 3$, and $8 − 3 = 5$.

greater: More

group: An amount more than 1

less: A smaller amount or number

number: The digits or units used for counting

number sentence: A math sentence that uses symbols of addition (+) or subtraction (−) and equals (=)

operation: The steps you take to work out a problem (+ or −)

regrouping: Taking a part of one number and giving it to another number to make a new group. $9 + 3$ can be regrouped by taking 1 away from the 3 and giving it to 9. Then the 9 becomes a 10 and you can add it to the 2 left over from the original 3. $10 + 2$ might be easier to add in your head than $9 + 3$.

solve: Find an answer

subtraction: Taking away an amount from another number

sum: The total amount after adding numbers together

zero: 1. Nothing. 2. A number used for important higher place values like 10, 100, 1,000

ANSWER KEY

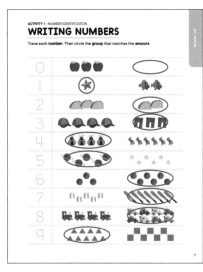

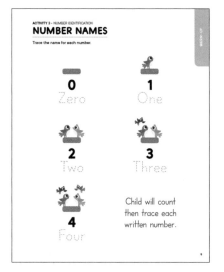

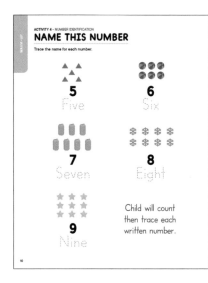

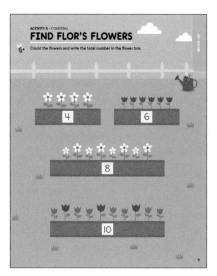

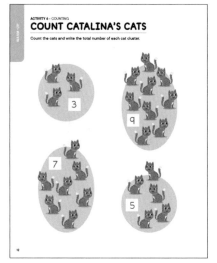

ACTIVITY 7 • NUMBER SEQUENCING
WRITE THE MISSING NUMBER
Write the missing number in the carts so the numbers are in order. Hint: Counting in order out loud will help you.

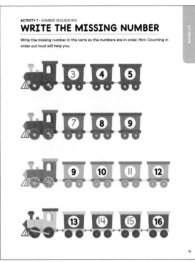

ACTIVITY 8 • NUMBER SEQUENCING
WHAT NUMBER IS MISSING?
Help Hana put her horses in order. Circle the correct number for the blank horse.

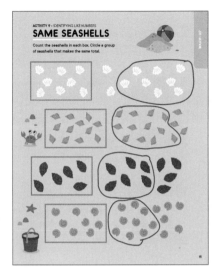

ACTIVITY 9 • IDENTIFYING LIKE NUMBERS
SAME SEASHELLS
Count the seashells in each box. Circle a group of seashells that makes the same total.

ACTIVITY 10 • IDENTIFYING LIKE NUMBERS
SAME STARS
Help Satoru find matching numbers of stars. Draw a line from one group of stars to another group with the same number of stars.

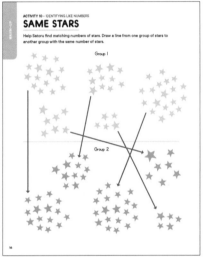

Group 1

Group 2

ACTIVITY 11 • CREATING LIKE NUMBERS
TALLY UP FARM
Draw tally marks for each number of animals shown.

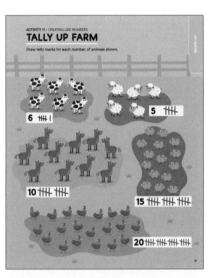

6 |||| |
5 ||||
10 |||| ||||
15 |||| |||| ||||
20 |||| |||| |||| ||||

ACTIVITY 12 • IDENTIFYING ZERO
ZERO THE HERO
Zero is an important number. By itself it means there is nothing, but zero can help other numbers become bigger! Help each number become bigger by writing in the zeroes for every number set.

_0_

1_0_   4_0_

2_0_   5_0_

3_0_

ACTIVITY 13 • COUNTING
COUNTING MY ALPHABET SOUP
Count how many times you see each letter in the bowl. Circle the letters as you count. Then write each total in the boxes below.

A	B	C	D	E
8	6	5	9	12

ACTIVITY 14 • COUNTING/COMBINING
TIME FOR 10
Circle groups of 10 bugs. The groups don't have to be all the same bug. Answers will vary.

Answers will vary.

ACTIVITY 15 • COUNTING/COMBINING
MAKE A TEN FRAME
Complete the ten frames. Write the number of dots you drew that helped to make 10.

4 + _6_ = 10   3 + _7_ = 10

5 + _5_ = 10   2 + _8_ = 10

8 + _2_ = 10   1 + _9_ = 10

129

ANSWER KEY

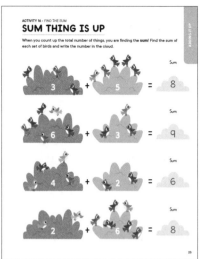

ACTIVITY 16 · FIND THE SUM
SUM THING IS UP

When you count up the total number of things, you are finding the **sum**! Find the sum of each set of birds and write the number in the cloud.

3 + 5 = 8
6 + 3 = 9
4 + 2 = 6
2 + 6 = 8

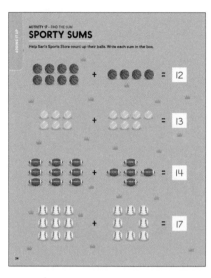

ACTIVITY 17 · FIND THE SUM
SPORTY SUMS

Help Sari's Sports Store count up their balls. Write each sum in the box.

+ = 12
+ = 13
+ = 14
+ = 17

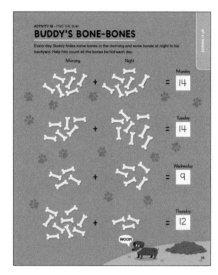

ACTIVITY 18 · FIND THE SUM
BUDDY'S BONE-BONES

Every day, Buddy hides some bones in the morning and some bones at night in his backyard. Help him count all the bones he hid each day.

Morning + Night

Monday = 14
Tuesday = 14
Wednesday = 9
Thursday = 12

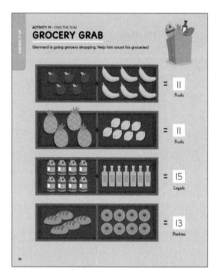

ACTIVITY 19 · FIND THE SUM
GROCERY GRAB

Glennard is going grocery shopping. Help him count his groceries!

+ = 11 Fruits
= 11 Fruits
= 15 Liquids
= 13 Pastries

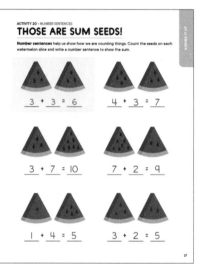

ACTIVITY 20 · NUMBER SENTENCES
THOSE ARE SUM SEEDS!

Number sentences help us show how we are counting things. Count the seeds on each watermelon slice and write a number sentence to show the sum.

3 + 3 = 6
4 + 3 = 7
3 + 7 = 10
7 + 2 = 9
1 + 4 = 5
3 + 2 = 5

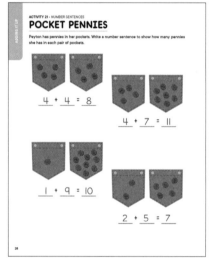

ACTIVITY 21 · NUMBER SENTENCES
POCKET PENNIES

Peyton has pennies in her pockets. Write a number sentence to show how many pennies she has in each pair of pockets.

4 + 4 = 8
4 + 7 = 11
1 + 9 = 10
2 + 5 = 7

ACTIVITY 22 · NUMBER SENTENCES
LET IT BEE

Binh has a bee farm. Help him count the bees and write a number sentence under each beehive box.

6 + 6 = 12
7 + 5 = 12
9 + 2 = 11
7 + 9 = 16

ACTIVITY 23 · NUMBER SENTENCES
PETTING ZOO

The numbers you add in an addition number sentence are called **addends**. For each group of animals, circle the two different types. Count how many there are of each type then write the addends in a number sentence to find the sum.

3 + 8 = 11
3 + 2 = 5
5 + 2 = 7
6 + 1 = 7

ACTIVITY 24 · NUMBER SENTENCES
LUNCH COUNT

Help the cafeteria crew add how many students are at each table. Write the number sentence for each table. Then circle the table with the largest number of students.

1 + 5 = 6
3 + 4 = 7
6 + 4 = 10

ACTIVITY 25 – NUMBER SENTENCES
THEODORE'S DOORS

Theodore's house has lots of interesting doors with shapes of different colors and sizes on them. Find the different types of shapes you see on each door. Then write an addition **equation** to show the total.

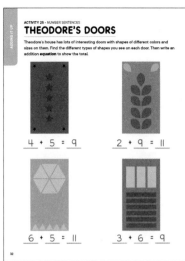

$4 + 5 = 9$

$2 + 9 = 11$

$6 + 5 = 11$

$3 + 6 = 9$

ACTIVITY 26 – NUMBER SENTENCES
YUKI'S KITCHEN

Yuki has lots of cooking tools. Find the sum of some of the tools in her kitchen.

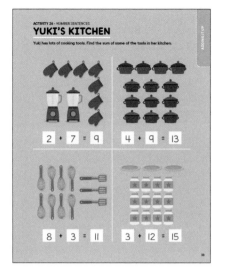

$2 + 7 = 9$

$4 + 9 = 13$

$8 + 3 = 11$

$3 + 12 = 15$

ACTIVITY 27 – NUMBER SENTENCES
CAROLYN'S CANDY SHOP

Carolyn is selling candy. Help her add up the coins above and below the center line to find the cost of each candy. Write the equation to show the sum.

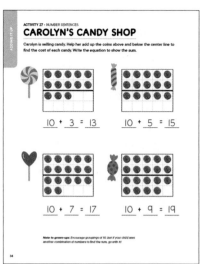

$10 + 3 = 13$

$10 + 5 = 15$

$10 + 7 = 17$

$10 + 9 = 19$

Note to grown-ups: Encourage groupings of 10, but if your child sees another combination of numbers to find the sum, go with it!

ACTIVITY 28 – FACT FAMILIES
DOTS ON DICE

Fact families are related number sentences that use the same numbers. Alma is rolling dice. For each pair of dice, draw in the number of dots Alma needs to make the number at the top.

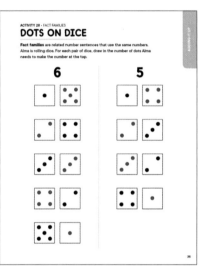

ACTIVITY 29 – FACT FAMILIES
MORE DOTS ON DICE

For each pair of dice, draw in the number of dots needed to make the number at the top.

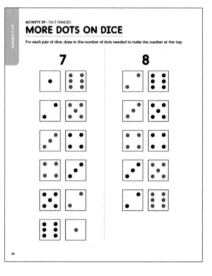

ACTIVITY 30 – FACT FAMILIES
TIME FOR TENS

Tak is making groups of tens. Help him by adding more dots to the ten frames, then write the equation that makes 10!

$1 + 9 = 10$

$3 + 7 = 10$

$9 + 1 = 10$

$7 + 3 = 10$

$2 + 8 = 10$

$4 + 6 = 10$

$8 + 2 = 10$

$6 + 4 = 10$

ACTIVITY 31 – FACT FAMILIES
WHAT PATTERN DO YOU SEE?

First count the number of blocks in each set. Then tell a grown-up a pattern you notice in the green and orange blocks. What pattern do you see in the blue and yellow blocks? How about the pink and red blocks?

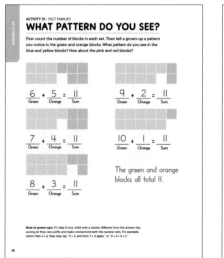

$\underset{\text{Green}}{6} + \underset{\text{Orange}}{5} = \underset{\text{Sum}}{11}$

$\underset{\text{Green}}{9} + \underset{\text{Orange}}{2} = \underset{\text{Sum}}{11}$

$\underset{\text{Green}}{7} + \underset{\text{Orange}}{4} = \underset{\text{Sum}}{11}$

$\underset{\text{Green}}{10} + \underset{\text{Orange}}{1} = \underset{\text{Sum}}{11}$

$\underset{\text{Green}}{8} + \underset{\text{Orange}}{3} = \underset{\text{Sum}}{11}$

The green and orange blocks all total 11.

Note to grown-ups: It's okay if your child sees a cluster different from the answer key, as long as they can justify and make connections with the number sets. For example, rather than 6 + 6, they may say: "3 + 3, and then 3 + 3 again," or "3 + 3 + 3 + 3."

$\underset{\text{Yellow}}{6} + \underset{\text{Blue}}{6} = \underset{\text{Sum}}{12}$

$\underset{\text{Pink}}{6} + \underset{\text{Red}}{7} = \underset{\text{Sum}}{13}$

$\underset{\text{Yellow}}{7} + \underset{\text{Blue}}{5} = \underset{\text{Sum}}{12}$

$\underset{\text{Pink}}{7} + \underset{\text{Red}}{6} = \underset{\text{Sum}}{13}$

$\underset{\text{Yellow}}{8} + \underset{\text{Blue}}{4} = \underset{\text{Sum}}{12}$

$\underset{\text{Pink}}{8} + \underset{\text{Red}}{5} = \underset{\text{Sum}}{13}$

$\underset{\text{Yellow}}{9} + \underset{\text{Blue}}{3} = \underset{\text{Sum}}{12}$

$\underset{\text{Pink}}{9} + \underset{\text{Red}}{4} = \underset{\text{Sum}}{13}$

$\underset{\text{Yellow}}{10} + \underset{\text{Blue}}{2} = \underset{\text{Sum}}{12}$

$\underset{\text{Pink}}{10} + \underset{\text{Red}}{3} = \underset{\text{Sum}}{13}$

The yellow and blue blocks all total 12.

The pink and red blocks all total 13.

ACTIVITY 32 – DOUBLES
PEPPERONI PIES

Count how many pieces of pepperoni are on each slice of pizza. What do you notice about each plate? That's right! When you see two things with the same amount, it's called a **double**! Write the doubles that sum up the pepperoni pieces.

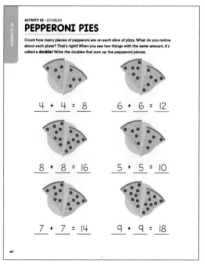

$4 + 4 = 8$

$6 + 6 = 12$

$8 + 8 = 16$

$5 + 5 = 10$

$7 + 7 = 14$

$9 + 9 = 18$

ANSWER KEY

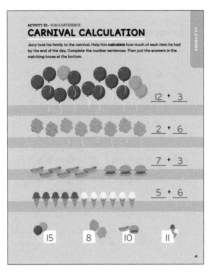

ACTIVITY 33 · SUM & DIFFERENCE
CARNIVAL CALCULATION

Jerry took his family to the carnival. Help him **calculate** how much of each item he had by the end of the day. Complete the number sentences. Then put the answers in the matching boxes at the bottom.

$12 + 3$

$2 + 6$

$7 + 3$

$5 + 6$

15   8   10   11

41

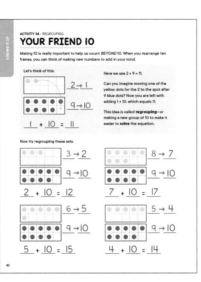

ACTIVITY 34 · REGROUPING
YOUR FRIEND 10

Making 10 is really important to help us count *BEYOND* 10. When you rearrange ten frames, you can think of making new numbers to add in your mind.

Let's think of this:

$2 \to 1$
$9 \to 10$

$1 + 10 = 11$

Here we see 2 + 9 = 11.

Can you imagine moving one of the yellow dots for the 2 to the spot after 9 blue dots? Now you are left with adding 1 + 10, which equals 11.

This idea is called **regrouping**—or making a new group of 10 to make it easier to **solve** the equation.

Now try regrouping these sets.

$3 \to 2$
$9 \to 10$
$2 + 10 = 12$

$8 \to 7$
$9 \to 10$
$7 + 10 = 17$

$6 \to 5$
$9 \to 10$
$5 + 10 = 15$

$5 \to 4$
$9 \to 10$
$4 + 10 = 14$

42

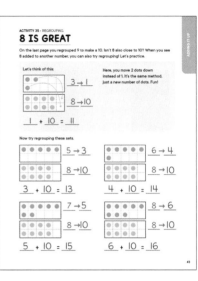

ACTIVITY 35 · REGROUPING
8 IS GREAT

On the last page you regrouped 9 to make a 10. Isn't 8 also close to 10? When you see 8 added to another number, you can also try regrouping! Let's practice.

Let's think of this:

$3 \to 1$
$8 \to 10$

$1 + 10 = 11$

Here, you move 2 dots down instead of 1. It's the same method. Just a new number of dots. Fun!

Now try regrouping these sets.

$5 \to 3$
$8 \to 10$
$3 + 10 = 13$

$6 \to 4$
$8 \to 10$
$4 + 10 = 14$

$7 \to 5$
$8 \to 10$
$5 + 10 = 15$

$8 \to 6$
$8 \to 10$
$6 + 10 = 16$

43

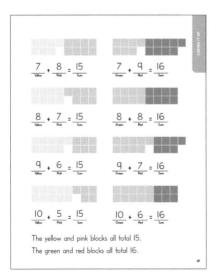

ACTIVITY 36 · PROBLEM-SOLVING
KYLE'S GAMES

Kyle played three games on the weekend. After the first game, he was sad because he didn't score any baskets. But he didn't give up! By the end of all three games, he had scored 30 baskets. How many baskets could he have scored in each of the last two games? Explain your thinking to a grown-up. Answers will vary.

Game 1	Game 2	Game 3
0		

Answers will vary

44

ACTIVITY 37 · NUMBER SENTENCES
DOGGY DANCE

Lilo is having a dog dance party! Help her count her dog friends in each group, then add them together in a number sentence.

$4 + 5 = 9$

$2 + 3 = 5$

$3 + 5 = 8$

$6 + 3 = 9$

45

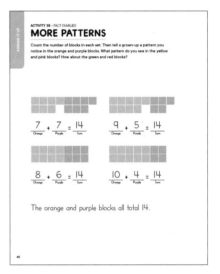

ACTIVITY 38 · FACT FAMILIES
MORE PATTERNS

Count the number of blocks in each set. Then tell a grown-up a pattern you notice in the orange and purple blocks. What pattern do you see in the yellow and pink blocks? How about the green and red blocks?

$\underset{\text{Orange}}{7} + \underset{\text{Purple}}{7} = \underset{\text{Sum}}{14}$

$\underset{\text{Orange}}{9} + \underset{\text{Purple}}{5} = \underset{\text{Sum}}{14}$

$\underset{\text{Orange}}{8} + \underset{\text{Purple}}{6} = \underset{\text{Sum}}{14}$

$\underset{\text{Orange}}{10} + \underset{\text{Purple}}{4} = \underset{\text{Sum}}{14}$

The orange and purple blocks all total 14.

46

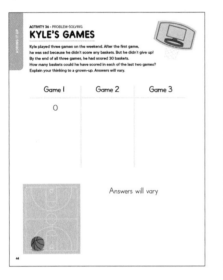

$\underset{\text{Yellow}}{7} + \underset{\text{Pink}}{8} = \underset{\text{Sum}}{15}$

$\underset{\text{Green}}{7} + \underset{\text{Red}}{9} = \underset{\text{Sum}}{16}$

$\underset{\text{Yellow}}{8} + \underset{\text{Pink}}{7} = \underset{\text{Sum}}{15}$

$\underset{\text{Green}}{8} + \underset{\text{Red}}{8} = \underset{\text{Sum}}{16}$

$\underset{\text{Yellow}}{9} + \underset{\text{Pink}}{6} = \underset{\text{Sum}}{15}$

$\underset{\text{Green}}{9} + \underset{\text{Red}}{7} = \underset{\text{Sum}}{16}$

$\underset{\text{Yellow}}{10} + \underset{\text{Pink}}{5} = \underset{\text{Sum}}{15}$

$\underset{\text{Green}}{10} + \underset{\text{Red}}{6} = \underset{\text{Sum}}{16}$

The yellow and pink blocks all total 15.
The green and red blocks all total 16.

47

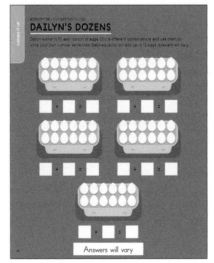

ACTIVITY 39 · NUMBER SENTENCES
DAILYN'S DOZENS

Dailyn wants to fill each carton of eggs. Circle different combinations and use them to write your own number sentences. Each equation will add up to 12 eggs. Answers will vary.

⬜ + ⬜ =

⬜ + ⬜ =

⬜ + ⬜ =

Answers will vary

48

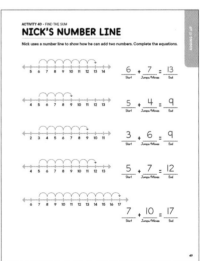

ACTIVITY 40 · FIND THE SUM
NICK'S NUMBER LINE

Nick uses a number line to show how he can add two numbers. Complete the equations.

$\underset{\text{Start}}{6} + \underset{\text{Jumps/Moves}}{7} = \underset{\text{End}}{13}$

$\underset{\text{Start}}{5} + \underset{\text{Jumps/Moves}}{4} = \underset{\text{End}}{9}$

$\underset{\text{Start}}{3} + \underset{\text{Jumps/Moves}}{6} = \underset{\text{End}}{9}$

$\underset{\text{Start}}{5} + \underset{\text{Jumps/Moves}}{7} = \underset{\text{End}}{12}$

$\underset{\text{Start}}{7} + \underset{\text{Jumps/Moves}}{10} = \underset{\text{End}}{17}$

49

ACTIVITY 41 · NUMBER SENTENCES
DEVONTE'S DOUGHNUTS

Help Devonte make different **combinations** of doughnuts. Create equations based on the types of doughnuts you see. Answers will vary.

___ + ___ = ___

___ + ___ = ___

___ + ___ = ___

___ + ___ = ___

___ + ___ = ___

Answers will vary

ACTIVITY 42 · NUMBER SENTENCES
CARNIVAL COUNTS

You are allowed to spend 15 dollars ($) on two items at the carnival! Which pairs of items can you buy so that you spend all $15?

$\underline{3} + \underline{12} = \underline{15}$

$\underline{5} + \underline{10} = \underline{15}$

$\underline{6} + \underline{9} = \underline{15}$

$\underline{7} + \underline{8} = \underline{15}$

ACTIVITY 43 · FACT FAMILIES
EVEN MORE PATTERNS

Count the number of blocks in each set. Then tell a grown-up a pattern you notice in the green and yellow blocks. What pattern do you see in the blue and pink blocks? How about the orange and red blocks?

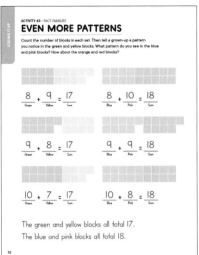

$\underline{8}_{\text{Green}} + \underline{9}_{\text{Yellow}} = \underline{17}_{\text{Sum}}$ $\underline{8}_{\text{Blue}} + \underline{10}_{\text{Pink}} = \underline{18}_{\text{Sum}}$

$\underline{9}_{\text{Green}} + \underline{8}_{\text{Yellow}} = \underline{17}_{\text{Sum}}$ $\underline{9}_{\text{Blue}} + \underline{9}_{\text{Pink}} = \underline{18}_{\text{Sum}}$

$\underline{10}_{\text{Green}} + \underline{7}_{\text{Yellow}} = \underline{17}_{\text{Sum}}$ $\underline{10}_{\text{Blue}} + \underline{8}_{\text{Pink}} = \underline{18}_{\text{Sum}}$

The green and yellow blocks all total 17.
The blue and pink blocks all total 18.

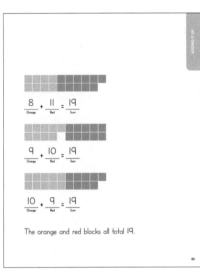

$\underline{8}_{\text{Orange}} + \underline{11}_{\text{Red}} = \underline{19}_{\text{Sum}}$

$\underline{9}_{\text{Orange}} + \underline{10}_{\text{Red}} = \underline{19}_{\text{Sum}}$

$\underline{10}_{\text{Orange}} + \underline{9}_{\text{Red}} = \underline{19}_{\text{Sum}}$

The orange and red blocks all total 19.

ACTIVITY 44 · NUMBER SENTENCES
BIRD BATH

For each fountain, choose two groups of birds, then write your addition equation. Answers will vary.

___ + ___ = ___

___ + ___ = ___

___ + ___ = ___

Answers will vary

ACTIVITY 45 · NUMBER SENTENCES
SPORT SORT

Choose combinations of balls and add them together! Answers will vary.

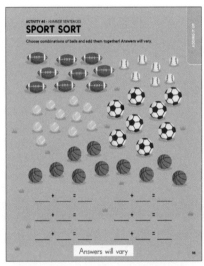

___ + ___ = ___

___ + ___ = ___

___ + ___ = ___

Answers will vary

Review/Practice

$1+1 = \underline{2}$ $1+2 = \underline{3}$

$2+2 = \underline{4}$ $2+3 = \underline{5}$

$3+3 = \underline{6}$ $3+4 = \underline{7}$

$4+4 = \underline{8}$ $4+5 = \underline{9}$

$5+5 = \underline{10}$ $5+6 = \underline{11}$

$6+6 = \underline{12}$ $6+7 = \underline{13}$

$7+7 = \underline{14}$ $7+8 = \underline{15}$

$8+8 = \underline{16}$ $8+9 = \underline{17}$

ACTIVITY 46 · FIND THE DIFFERENCE
BYE-BYE, BIRDIES

When you count down by taking away from the total, you are finding the **difference!** Find the difference of each set of birds and write the number in the cloud.

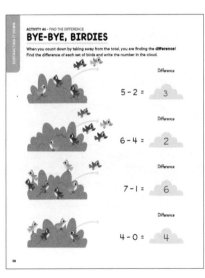

Difference
$5 - 2 = \underline{3}$

Difference
$6 - 4 = \underline{2}$

Difference
$7 - 1 = \underline{6}$

Difference
$4 - 0 = \underline{4}$

ACTIVITY 47 · FIND THE DIFFERENCE
LISA'S PIZZA

Lisa ate some pizza slices. How many slices of pizza remain on each plate?

$\underline{4}_{\text{Slices}} - \underline{3}_{\text{Eaten}} = \underline{1}_{\text{Remain}}$ $\underline{6}_{\text{Slices}} - \underline{2}_{\text{Eaten}} = \underline{4}_{\text{Remain}}$

$\underline{8}_{\text{Slices}} - \underline{2}_{\text{Eaten}} = \underline{6}_{\text{Remain}}$ $\underline{8}_{\text{Slices}} - \underline{5}_{\text{Eaten}} = \underline{3}_{\text{Remain}}$

ANSWER KEY

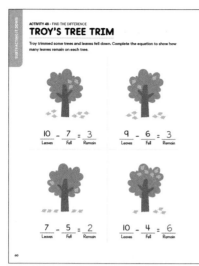

ACTIVITY 48 · FIND THE DIFFERENCE

TROY'S TREE TRIM

Troy trimmed some trees and leaves fell down. Complete the equation to show how many leaves remain on each tree.

$$10 - 7 = 3$$
Leaves Fell Remain

$$9 - 6 = 3$$
Leaves Fell Remain

$$7 - 5 = 2$$
Leaves Fell Remain

$$10 - 4 = 6$$
Leaves Fell Remain

60

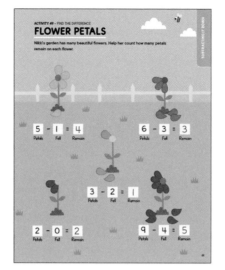

ACTIVITY 49 · FIND THE DIFFERENCE

FLOWER PETALS

Nikki's garden has many beautiful flowers. Help her count how many petals remain on each flower.

$$5 - 1 = 4$$
Petals Fell Remain

$$6 - 3 = 3$$
Petals Fell Remain

$$3 - 2 = 1$$
Petals Fell Remain

$$2 - 0 = 2$$
Petals Fell Remain

$$9 - 4 = 5$$
Petals Fell Remain

61

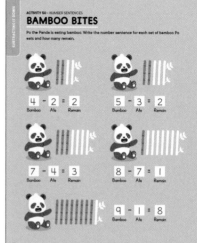

ACTIVITY 50 · NUMBER SENTENCES

BAMBOO BITES

Po the Panda is eating bamboo. Write the number sentence for each set of bamboo Po eats and how many remain.

$$4 - 2 = 2$$
Bamboo Ate Remain

$$5 - 3 = 2$$
Bamboo Ate Remain

$$7 - 4 = 3$$
Bamboo Ate Remain

$$8 - 7 = 1$$
Bamboo Ate Remain

$$9 - 1 = 8$$
Bamboo Ate Remain

62

ACTIVITY 51 · NUMBER SENTENCES

LET'S TACO 'BOUT IT

Tanya's family eats tacos every weekday this week. Tanya eats some, then gives the rest to her sister. For each day, how many tacos does she have left to give to her sister?

MONDAY
$$3 - 1 = 2$$
Tacos Ate For sister

TUESDAY
$$4 - 4 = 0$$
Tacos Ate For sister

WEDNESDAY
$$5 - 0 = 5$$
Tacos Ate For sister

THURSDAY
$$7 - 6 = 1$$
Tacos Ate For sister

FRIDAY
$$8 - 4 = 4$$
Tacos Ate For sister

63

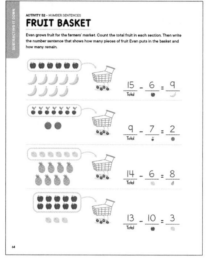

ACTIVITY 52 · NUMBER SENTENCES

FRUIT BASKET

Evan grows fruit for the farmers' market. Count the total fruit in each section. Then write the number sentence that shows how many pieces of fruit Evan puts in the basket and how many remain.

$$15 - 6 = 9$$
Total

$$9 - 7 = 2$$
Total

$$14 - 6 = 8$$
Total

$$13 - 10 = 3$$
Total

64

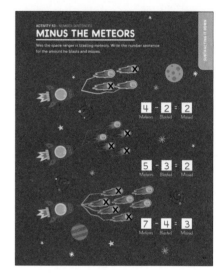

ACTIVITY 53 · NUMBER SENTENCES

MINUS THE METEORS

Was the space ranger is blasting meteors. Write the number sentence for the amount he blasts and misses.

$$4 - 2 = 2$$
Meteors Blasted Missed

$$5 - 3 = 2$$
Meteors Blasted Missed

$$7 - 4 = 3$$
Meteors Blasted Missed

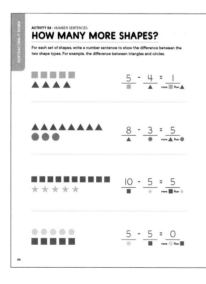

ACTIVITY 54 · NUMBER SENTENCES

HOW MANY MORE SHAPES?

For each set of shapes, write a number sentence to show the difference between the two shape types. For example, the difference between triangles and circles.

$$5 - 4 = 1$$
■ ▲ more ■ than ▲

$$8 - 3 = 5$$
▲ ● more ▲ than ●

$$10 - 5 = 5$$
■ ★ more ■ than ★

$$5 - 5 = 0$$
● ■ more ● than ■

66

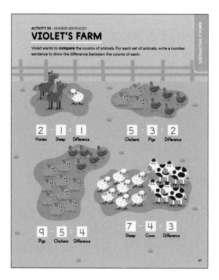

ACTIVITY 55 · NUMBER SENTENCES

VIOLET'S FARM

Violet wants to **compare** the counts of animals. For each set of animals, write a number sentence to show the difference between the counts of each.

$$2 - 1 = 1$$
Horses Sheep Difference

$$5 - 3 = 2$$
Chickens Pigs Difference

$$9 - 5 = 4$$
Pigs Chickens Difference

$$7 - 4 = 3$$
Sheep Cows Difference

67

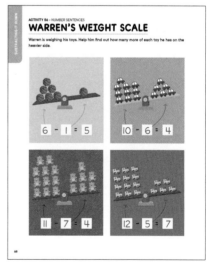

ACTIVITY 56 · NUMBER SENTENCES

WARREN'S WEIGHT SCALE

Warren is weighing his toys. Help him find out how many more of each toy he has on the heavier side.

$$6 - 1 = 5$$

$$10 - 6 = 4$$

$$11 - 7 = 4$$

$$12 - 5 = 7$$

68

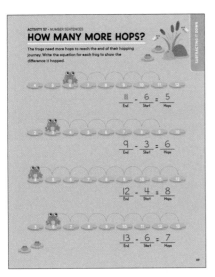

ACTIVITY 57 - NUMBER SENTENCES
HOW MANY MORE HOPS?

The frogs need more hops to reach the end of their hopping journey. Write the equation for each frog to show the difference it hopped.

$$\underset{\text{End}}{11} - \underset{\text{Start}}{6} = \underset{\text{Hops}}{5}$$

$$\underset{\text{End}}{9} - \underset{\text{Start}}{3} = \underset{\text{Hops}}{6}$$

$$\underset{\text{End}}{12} - \underset{\text{Start}}{4} = \underset{\text{Hops}}{8}$$

$$\underset{\text{End}}{13} - \underset{\text{Start}}{6} = \underset{\text{Hops}}{7}$$

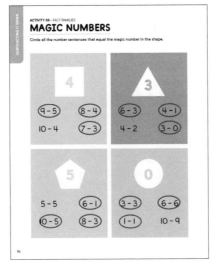

ACTIVITY 58 - FACT FAMILIES
MAGIC NUMBERS

Circle all the number sentences that equal the magic number in the shape.

4
(9 - 5) (8 - 4)
10 - 4 (7 - 3)

3
(6 - 3) (4 - 1)
4 - 2 (3 - 0)

5
5 - 5 (6 - 1)
(0 - 5) (8 - 3)

0
(3 - 3) (6 - 6)
(1 - 1) 10 - 9

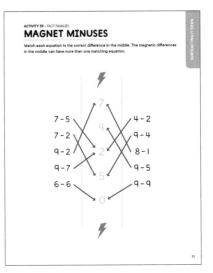

ACTIVITY 59 - FACT FAMILIES
MAGNET MINUSES

Match each equation to the correct difference in the middle. The magnetic differences in the middle can have more than one matching equation.

7 - 5   7
7 - 2   4   4 - 2
9 - 2   2   9 - 4
9 - 7   5   8 - 1
6 - 6   0   9 - 5
                    9 - 9

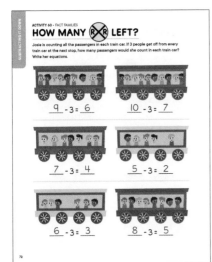

ACTIVITY 60 - FACT FAMILIES
HOW MANY R⊗R LEFT?

Josie is counting all the passengers in each train car. If 3 people get off from every train car at the next stop, how many passengers would she count in each train car? Write her equations.

9 - 3 = 6   10 - 3 = 7

7 - 3 = 4   5 - 3 = 2

6 - 3 = 3   8 - 3 = 5

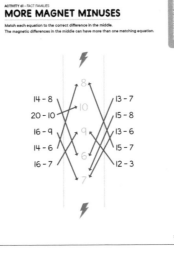

ACTIVITY 61 - FACT FAMILIES
MORE MAGNET MINUSES

Match each equation to the correct difference in the middle. The magnetic differences in the middle can have more than one matching equation.

14 - 8   8   13 - 7
20 - 10   10   15 - 8
16 - 9   9   13 - 6
14 - 6   6   15 - 7
16 - 7   7   12 - 3

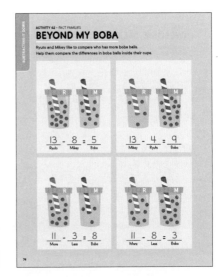

ACTIVITY 62 - FACT FAMILIES
BEYOND MY BOBA

Ryuto and Mikey like to compare who has more boba balls. Help them compare the differences in boba balls inside their cups.

$$\underset{\text{Ryuto}}{13} - \underset{\text{Mikey}}{8} = \underset{\text{Boba}}{5}$$

$$\underset{\text{Mikey}}{13} - \underset{\text{Ryuto}}{4} = \underset{\text{Boba}}{9}$$

$$\underset{\text{More}}{11} - \underset{\text{Less}}{3} = \underset{\text{Boba}}{8}$$

$$\underset{\text{More}}{11} - \underset{\text{Less}}{8} = \underset{\text{Boba}}{3}$$

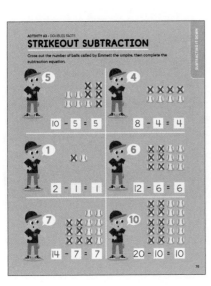

ACTIVITY 63 - DOUBLES FACTS
STRIKEOUT SUBTRACTION

Cross out the number of balls called by Emmett the umpire, then complete the subtraction equation.

5: 10 - 5 = 5
4: 8 - 4 = 4
1: 2 - 1 = 1
6: 12 - 6 = 6
7: 14 - 7 = 7
10: 20 - 10 = 10

ACTIVITY 64 - DOUBLES FACTS
HALF THE BOOKS

Knowing your doubles facts in addition is just as important in subtraction! Look at the double stacks of books and complete the fact family triangle and equation.

12 - 6 = 6   16 - 8 = 8

14 - 7 = 7   18 - 9 = 9

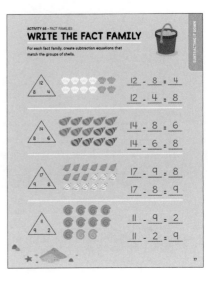

ACTIVITY 65 - FACT FAMILIES
WRITE THE FACT FAMILY

For each fact family, create subtraction equations that match the groups of shells.

12 - 8 = 4
12 - 4 = 8

14 - 8 = 6
14 - 6 = 8

17 - 9 = 8
17 - 8 = 9

11 - 9 = 2
11 - 2 = 9

ACTIVITY 66 · REGROUPING
HANG 10

Emi likes to take at least 10 steps while she's riding her surfboard.
The numbers on the board show how many steps she took.
On the lines show how many more steps she took past 10.

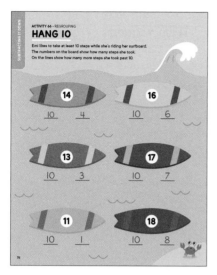

14 → 10   4
16 → 10   6
13 → 10   3
17 → 10   7
11 → 10   1
18 → 10   8

ACTIVITY 67 · REGROUPING
SUBTRACT FROM 10

When big numbers are tricky to subtract, try to break one of the numbers into friendly numbers like 10.

For 13 − 5, think of 13 as 10 and 3.
Then take 5 away from 10.
You're left with 5 and 3, which is 8!
So, 13 − 5 = 8.

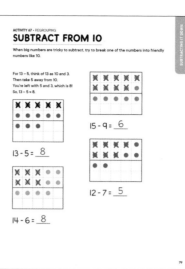

13 − 5 = 8
15 − 9 = 6
14 − 6 = 8
12 − 7 = 5

ACTIVITY 68 · NUMBER SENTENCES
COMPARING CONES

Ruby is comparing which ice cream flavors sold today in her ice cream shop. First color in the squares that match the number of ice cream flavors she sold. Then help her find the differences between the flavors she sold.

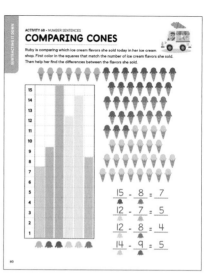

15 − 8 = 7
12 − 7 = 5
12 − 8 = 4
14 − 9 = 5

ACTIVITY 69 · NUMBER SENTENCES
AWESOME OLLIES

Wilder ollies (jumps) over the line of cones. Help Wilder complete the subtraction sentences to show how many cones he jumps and the number he lands on.

3 − 2 = 1
7 − 6 = 1
10 − 4 = 6
9 − 5 = 4

ACTIVITY 70 · COMPARING/NUMBER SENTENCES
DEREK'S DONATION

Solve the problems below and explain to a grown-up how you did it.

Derek had 15 toys he didn't need anymore. He donated 9 toys and gave the rest to his sister, Althea. How many toys did Althea get?

15 − 9 = 6
Total toys   Donated   Althea's toys

The 9 toys that Derek donated went to a new boy named Miles. Miles painted 6 of the toys. How many toys were not painted?

9 − 6 = 3
Donated   Painted   Not painted

ACTIVITY 71 · NUMBER SENTENCES
SHOPPING TIME

Ryan bought some new items. Cross out the number of dollars he used for each item and complete the subtraction equation.

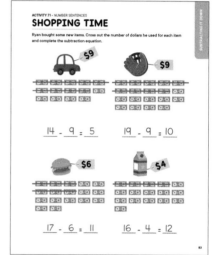

$9 $9
14 − 9 = 5   19 − 9 = 10

$6 $4
17 − 6 = 11   16 − 4 = 12

ACTIVITY 72 · COMPARING/NUMBER SENTENCES
FISHING FUN

Use the pictures to help you solve the problem. Explain your thinking to a grown-up.

Olivia and Zoey went fishing in a pond with 17 red fish and 14 purple fish. Olivia caught 8 red fish and Zoey caught 5 purple fish. Olivia said she left more fish in the pond. Zoey said they left the same amount. Who's right? Why?

Show your thinking here:
Zoey is correct: 9 red fish and
9 purple fish remain in the pond.
17−8=9 (Olivia) 14−5=9 (Zoey)

ACTIVITY 73 · NUMBER SENTENCES
FLY AWAY FEATHERS

Count the birds in each tree. Draw an X to cross out how many you want to fly away. Then make a subtraction equation. Answers will vary.

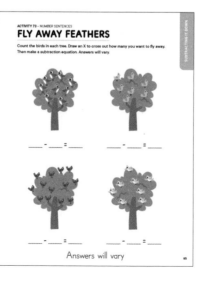

____ − ____ = ____   ____ − ____ = ____

____ − ____ = ____   ____ − ____ = ____

Answers will vary

ACTIVITY 74 · NUMBER SENTENCES
BOWLING BUDDIES

Lindsey and Lani bowled three rounds. For each round, use subtraction to show how many pins they had left at the end of each round.

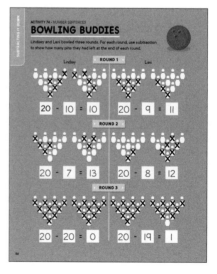

Lindsey   Lani
ROUND 1
20 − 10 = 10   20 − 9 = 11
ROUND 2
20 − 7 = 13   20 − 8 = 12
ROUND 3
20 − 20 = 0   20 − 19 = 1

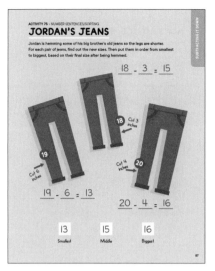

JORDAN'S JEANS

Jordan is hemming some of his big brother's old jeans so the legs are shorter. For each pair of jeans, find out the new sizes. Then put them in order from smallest to biggest, based on their final size after being hemmed.

$18 - 3 = 15$

$19 - 6 = 13$

$20 - 4 = 16$

13	15	16
Smallest	Middle	Biggest

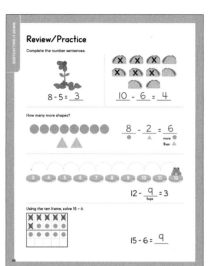

Review/Practice

Complete the number sentences.

$8 - 5 = 3$

$10 - 6 = 4$

How many more shapes?

$8 - 2 = 6$ more than

$12 - 9 = 3$ hops

Using the ten frame, solve 15 – 6.

$15 - 6 = 9$

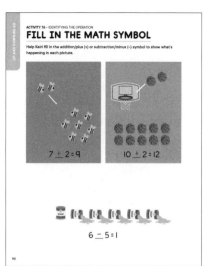

FILL IN THE MATH SYMBOL

Help Keiri fill in the addition/plus (+) or subtraction/minus (–) symbol to show what's happening in each picture.

$7 + 2 = 9$

$10 + 2 = 12$

$6 - 5 = 1$

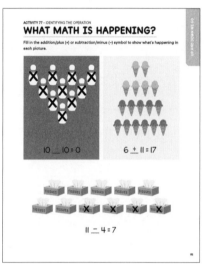

WHAT MATH IS HAPPENING?

Fill in the addition/plus (+) or subtraction/minus (–) symbol to show what's happening in each picture.

$10 - 10 = 0$

$6 + 11 = 17$

$11 - 4 = 7$

WHAT'S THE MATH?

Fill in the addition/plus (+) or subtraction/minus (–) symbol to show what's happening in each picture.

$6 - 4 = 2$

$13 - 4 = 9$

$11 + 4 = 15$

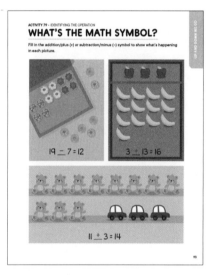

WHAT'S THE MATH SYMBOL?

Fill in the addition/plus (+) or subtraction/minus (–) symbol to show what's happening in each picture.

$19 - 7 = 12$

$3 + 13 = 16$

$11 + 3 = 14$

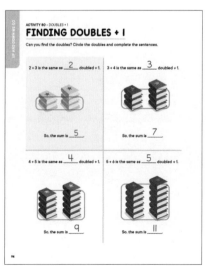

FINDING DOUBLES + 1

Can you find the doubles? Circle the doubles and complete the sentences.

2 + 3 is the same as 2 doubled + 1.

3 + 4 is the same as 3 doubled + 1.

So, the sum is 5

So, the sum is 7

4 + 5 is the same as 4 doubled + 1.

5 + 6 is the same as 5 doubled + 1.

So, the sum is 9

So, the sum is 11

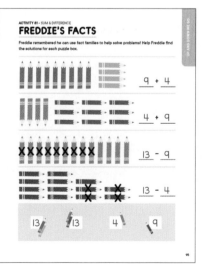

FREDDIE'S FACTS

Freddie remembered he can use fact families to help solve problems! Help Freddie find the solutions for each puzzle box.

$9 + 4$

$4 + 9$

$13 - 9$

$13 - 4$

13	13	4	9

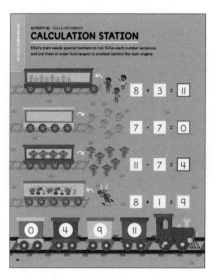

CALCULATION STATION

Elliot's train needs special numbers to run. Solve each number sentence and put them in order from largest to smallest behind the train engine.

$8 + 3 = 11$

$7 - 7 = 0$

$11 - 7 = 4$

$8 + 1 = 9$

0	4	9	11

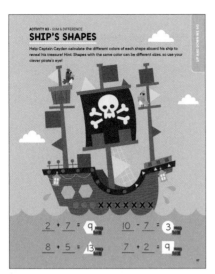

ACTIVITY 83 · SUM & DIFFERENCE

SHIP'S SHAPES

Help Captain Cayden calculate the different colors of each shape aboard his ship to reveal his treasure! Hint: Shapes with the same color can be different sizes, so use your clever pirate's eye!

$2 + 7 = 9$ $10 - 7 = 3$

$8 + 5 = 13$ $7 + 2 = 9$

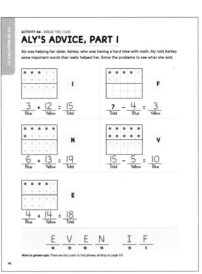

ACTIVITY 84 · BREAK THE CODE

ALY'S ADVICE, PART 1

Aly was helping her sister, Ashley, who was having a hard time with math. Aly told Ashley some important words that really helped her. Solve the problems to see what she said.

I
$3 + 12 = 15$
Blue   Yellow   Total

F
$7 - 4 = 3$
Total   Blue   Yellow

N
$6 + 13 = 19$
Blue   Yellow   Total

V
$15 - 5 = 10$
Total   Yellow   Blue

E
$4 + 14 = 18$
Blue   Yellow   Total

E V E N   I F
18 10 18 19   15 3

Note to grown-ups: There are four parts to this phrase, ending on page XII.

ACTIVITY 85 · BREAK THE CODE

ALY'S ADVICE, PART 2

Solve the problems to continue seeing what Aly said to Ashley.

$2 + 4 = 6$ T
$3 + 1 = 4$ R
$5 - 2 = 3$ H
$9 - 8 = 1$ I
$11 - 3 = 8$ A
$3 + 10 = 13$ S
$12 - 10 = 2$ N
$9 + 11 = 20$ D

I T   I S   H A R D
1 6   1 13   3 8 4 20

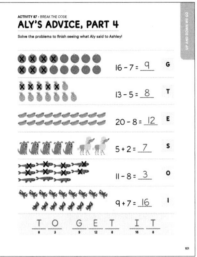

ACTIVITY 86 · BREAK THE CODE

ALY'S ADVICE, PART 3

Solve the problems to continue seeing what Aly said to Ashley.

$8 + 6 = 14$ $1 - 0 = 1$ $10 - 8 = 2$
A   W   D

$7 + 2 = 9$ $11 - 5 = 6$ $12 - 5 = 7$
R   H   E

$8 - 0 = 8$ $8 - 5 = 3$ $2 + 8 = 10$
O   U   K

W O R K
1 8 9 10

H A R D E R
6 14 9 7 2 9

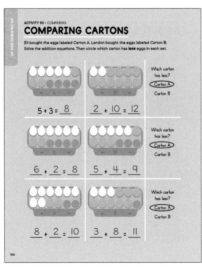

ACTIVITY 87 · BREAK THE CODE

ALY'S ADVICE, PART 4

Solve the problems to finish seeing what Aly said to Ashley!

$16 - 7 = 9$ G
$13 - 5 = 8$ T
$20 - 8 = 12$ E
$5 + 2 = 7$ S
$11 - 8 = 3$ O
$9 + 7 = 16$ I

T O   G E T   I T
8 3   9 12 8   16 8

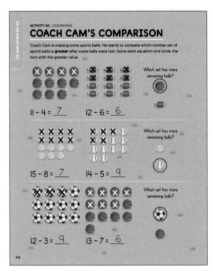

ACTIVITY 88 · COMPARING

COACH CAM'S COMPARISON

Coach Cam is missing some sports balls. He wants to compare which number set of sports balls is **greater** after some balls were lost. Solve each equation and circle the item with the greater value.

Which set has more remaining balls?

$11 - 4 = 7$ $12 - 6 = 6$

Which set has more remaining balls?

$15 - 8 = 7$ $14 - 5 = 9$

Which set has more remaining balls?

$12 - 3 = 9$ $13 - 7 = 6$

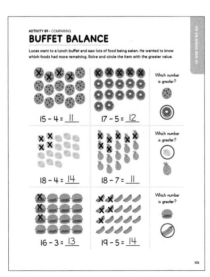

ACTIVITY 89 · COMPARING

BUFFET BALANCE

Lucas went to a lunch buffet and saw lots of food being eaten. He wanted to know which foods had more remaining. Solve and circle the item with the greater value.

Which number is greater?

$15 - 4 = 11$ $17 - 5 = 12$

Which number is greater?

$18 - 4 = 14$ $18 - 7 = 11$

Which number is greater?

$16 - 3 = 13$ $19 - 5 = 14$

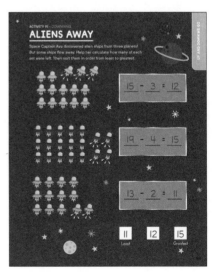

ACTIVITY 90 · COMPARING

COMPARING CARTONS

Eli bought the eggs labeled Carton A. Landon bought the eggs labeled Carton B. Solve the addition equations. Then circle which carton has **less** eggs in each set.

Which carton has less?
(Carton A)
Carton B

$5 + 3 = 8$ $2 + 10 = 12$

Which carton has less?
(Carton A)
Carton B

$6 + 2 = 8$ $5 + 4 = 9$

Which carton has less?
(Carton B)
Carton B

$8 + 2 = 10$ $3 + 8 = 11$

ACTIVITY 91 · COMPARING

ALIENS AWAY

Space Captain Ava discovered alien ships from three planets! But some ships flew away. Help her calculate how many of each set were left. Then sort them in order from least to greatest.

$15 - 3 = 12$

$19 - 4 = 15$

$13 - 2 = 11$

11 (Least)   12   15 (Greatest)

ACTIVITY 92 • NUMBER LINE
BUILDING BUDDIES

Four friends work in the same building and take the elevator up and down the floors. Number all the floors. Then use number sentences to show where they go.

If **Avery** goes down 5 floors, what floor will she be on? _15_ th floor
Show a number sentence that can help you.

$$20 - 5 = 15$$

If **Braxton** goes down 9 floors, what floor will she be on? _3_ rd floor
Show a number sentence that can help you.

$$12 - 9 = 3$$

If **Dahlia** goes up 5 floors, what floor will she be on? _12_ th floor
Show a number sentence that can help you.

$$7 + 5 = 12$$

If **Jasmine** goes up 9 floors, what floor will she be on? _16_ th floor
Show a number sentence that can help you.

$$7 + 9 = 16$$

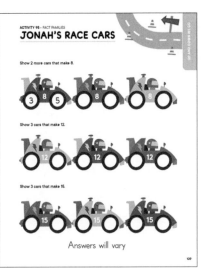

Floor
20, 19, 18, 17, 16, 15, 14, 13, 12, 11, 10, 9, 8, 7, 6, 5, 4, 3, 2, 1

Avery → 20
Braxton → 12
Dahlia and Jasmine → 7

106

ACTIVITY 93 • CREATE EQUATIONS
BROOKLYN'S BROOK

Brooklyn caught some fish. For each type of fish, cross out a group that she caught. Then write a subtraction sentence for that group of fish. Answers will vary.

Answers will vary

107

ACTIVITY 94 • CREATE EQUATIONS
ABBY'S ZOO

Abby the zookeeper is rounding up animals to put them to bed. Circle each set of animals. Write the total number of animals in each set. Then add the sets together so Abby can put the right number of animals to bed.

$$9 + 9 = 18$$

$$12 + 12 = 24$$

$$8 + 10 = 18$$

108

ACTIVITY 95 • FACT FAMILIES
JONAH'S RACE CARS

Show 2 more cars that make 8.

Show 3 cars that make 12.

Show 3 cars that make 15.

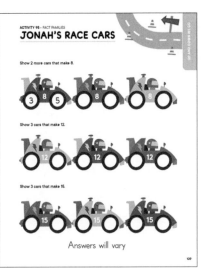

Answers will vary

109

ACTIVITY 96 • TRUE OR FALSE
TRUE OR FALSE?

Write T if the statement is true. Write F if it is false.

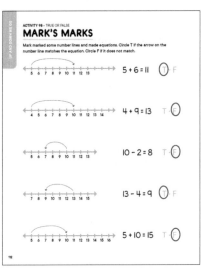

is greater than — T
6 + 10   2 + 11

is less than — T
10 + 4   5 + 12

is greater than — F
6 + 3   7 + 5

110

ACTIVITY 97 • NUMBER SENTENCES/COMPARING
KAYLIE'S COSTS

Kaylie is shopping and wants to know which combination of clothes costs more or less. Help her calculate and circle the item or group of items that is less so that she can save money!

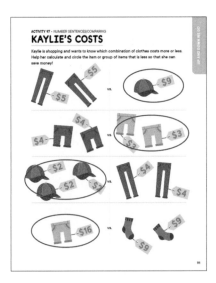

$5 $5   vs. $9 (circled)

$4 $4 vs. $3 $2 (circled)

$2 $2 $2 (circled) vs. $4 $4

$16 (circled) vs. $9 $9

111

ACTIVITY 98 • TRUE OR FALSE
MARK'S MARKS

Mark marked some number lines and made equations. Circle T if the arrow on the number line matches the equation. Circle F if it does not match.

5 + 6 = 11   (T) F

4 + 9 = 13   T (F)

10 - 2 = 8   T (F)

13 - 4 = 9   (T) F

5 + 10 = 15   T (F)

112

ACTIVITY 99 • STORY PROBLEMS
KEIRA'S PIE PROBLEM

Solve each problem below in a way that makes sense to you. Explain to a grown-up how you thought about it.

Keira made 14 pies for her party. At the end of the party, 3 pies were left. How many pies got eaten?   _11_

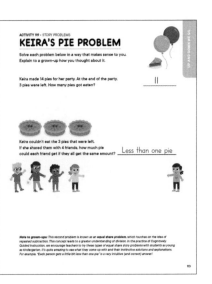

Keira couldn't eat the 3 pies that were left. If she shared them with 4 friends, how much pie could each friend get if they all get the same amount?   _Less than one pie_

Note to grown-ups: This second problem is known as an **equal share problem**, which touches on the idea of *repeated subtraction*. This concept leads to a greater understanding of division. In the practice of *Cognitively Guided Instruction*, we encourage teachers to try these type of equal share story problems with students as young as kindergarten. It's quite amazing to see what they come up with and their instinctive solutions and explanations. For example, "Each person gets a little bit less than one pie" is a very intuitive (and correct) answer!

113

ACTIVITY 100 • STORY PROBLEMS
PEARL'S PIGGY BANK

Solve the problems in a way that makes sense to you. Explain to a grown-up how you thought about it.

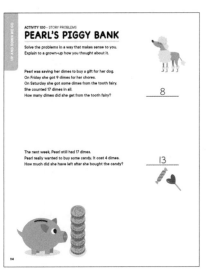

Pearl was saving her dimes to buy a gift for her dog. On Friday she got 9 dimes for her chores. On Saturday she got some dimes from the tooth fairy. She counted 17 dimes in all. How many dimes did she get from the tooth fairy?   _8_

The next week, Pearl still had 17 dimes. Pearl really wanted to buy some candy. It cost 4 dimes. How much did she have left after she bought the candy?   _13_

114

Review/Practice

15 − 3 = 12 Animals

9 − 3 = 6 Dollars left

12 − 8 = 4 Dollars left

8 + 14 = 22 Fish

Which is greater? (9 + 3) or 8 + 2

Which is less? (8 − 6) or 9 − 4

TIMED TEST #1 · 4 MINUTES
0-5 ADDITION

0+0= 0	0+1= 1	0+2= 2
3+0= 3	4+0= 4	5+0= 5
1+1= 2	1+2= 3	1+3= 4
2+1= 3	2+2= 4	2+3= 5
3+1= 4	4+1= 5	5+1= 6
3+3= 6	4+4= 8	5+5= 10
1+5= 6	5+3= 8	4+5= 9
5+4= 9	2+5= 7	3+4= 7
4+2= 6	5+1= 6	2+4= 6
4+0= 4	3+1= 4	2+2= 4
1+3= 4	0+4= 4	2+0= 2
1+0= 1	0+5= 5	0+3= 3
4+1= 5	1+2= 3	1+1= 2
2+0= 2	5+2= 7	4+3= 7
2+1= 3	3+0= 3	3+2= 5

TIMED TEST #2 · 3 MINUTES
0-5 ADDITION

5+0= 5	1+0= 1	0+5= 5
1+2= 3	0+2= 2	2+2= 4
4+1= 5	5+0= 5	0+0= 0
0+1= 1	3+1= 4	3+2= 5
3+5= 8	1+1= 2	1+2= 3
1+5= 6	2+4= 6	5+2= 7
4+3= 7	3+0= 3	0+4= 4
1+4= 5	0+3= 3	1+0= 1
0+1= 1	5+3= 8	5+5= 10
2+0= 2	0+0= 0	3+5= 8
1+3= 4	0+2= 2	0+3= 3
5+2= 7	2+0= 2	1+1= 2
4+4= 8	3+3= 6	0+0= 0
2+2= 4	1+1= 2	0+5= 5
1+4= 5	3+0= 3	2+1= 3

TIMED TEST #3 · 4 MINUTES
0-10 ADDITION

6+4= 10	7+3= 10	8+2= 10
9+1= 10	10+0= 10	1+8= 9
2+7= 9	3+6= 9	0+8= 8
6+1= 7	7+0= 7	6+0= 6
3+10= 13	1+10= 11	4+10= 14
6+3= 9	2+6= 8	10+2= 12
9+0= 9	6+8= 14	8+4= 12
4+9= 13	7+4= 11	7+2= 9
8+0= 8	0+7= 7	6+0= 6
0+9= 9	0+6= 6	7+5= 12
8+5= 13	8+3= 11	9+3= 12
8+1= 9	7+1= 8	9+4= 13
7+6= 13	5+8= 13	10+3= 13
10+1= 11	10+2= 12	4+6= 10
4+8= 12	9+2= 11	8+3= 11

TIMED TEST #4 · 3 MINUTES
0-10 ADDITION

10+1= 11	9+2= 11	8+3= 11
3+7= 10	4+6= 10	6+4= 10
5+5= 10	0+6= 6	7+1= 8
9+5= 14	10+6= 16	8+6= 14
9+6= 15	6+2= 8	7+5= 12
6+5= 11	1+9= 10	2+8= 10
8+5= 13	5+7= 12	6+10= 16
10+4= 14	0+10= 10	1+10= 11
3+9= 12	4+7= 11	9+7= 16
8+1= 9	8+0= 8	7+9= 16
2+9= 11	0+8= 8	8+9= 17
9+4= 13	7+6= 13	6+2= 8
8+6= 14	9+5= 14	3+8= 11
4+7= 11	7+0= 7	10+7= 17
10+8= 18	6+9= 15	5+8= 13

TIMED TEST #5 · 4 MINUTES
0-10 SUBTRACTION

0-0= 0	2-1= 1	3-1= 2
3-1= 2	5-1= 4	4-0= 4
5-2= 3	4-4= 0	5-4= 1
5-0= 5	6-5= 1	7-2= 5
8-7= 1	8-1= 7	7-1= 6
7-7= 0	8-8= 0	7-6= 1
9-9= 0	10-10= 0	9-6= 3
8-6= 2	6-0= 6	7-0= 7
0-0= 0	2-0= 2	2-2= 0
7-3= 4	6-2= 4	5-1= 4
3-0= 3	4-1= 3	6-3= 3
6-4= 1	6-5= 1	9-5= 4
7-3= 4	8-7= 1	8-3= 5
9-3= 6	10-4= 6	11-5= 6
10-6= 4	10-9= 1	6-4= 2

TIMED TEST #6 · 3 MINUTES
0-10 SUBTRACTION

10-5= 5	9-4= 5	8-3= 5
8-6= 2	9-8= 1	9-7= 2
4-3= 1	5-4= 1	1-1= 0
1-0= 1	6-0= 6	3-3= 0
7-5= 2	6-1= 5	7-6= 1
7-7= 0	9-0= 9	9-9= 0
9-5= 4	8-4= 4	8-3= 5
5-2= 3	6-4= 2	2-1= 1
3-2= 1	10-6= 4	4-1= 3
10-4= 6	13-8= 5	7-6= 1
8-7= 1	9-4= 5	6-2= 4
4-4= 0	10-8= 2	10-9= 1
10-7= 3	9-6= 3	12-9= 3
6-2= 4	5-5= 0	3-3= 0
5-3= 2	7-5= 2	7-4= 3

TIMED TEST #7 · 4 MINUTES
0-20 SUBTRACTION

7-0= 7	8-0= 8	9-0= 9
10-0= 10	9-1= 8	10-1= 9
11-3= 8	11-2= 9	11-1= 10
15-5= 10	15-6= 9	15-7= 8
13-8= 8	12-7= 7	11-6= 5
9-1= 8	12-4= 8	15-7= 8
17-9= 8	18-9= 9	19-9= 10
14-8= 6	13-7= 6	12-6= 6
12-8= 4	12-5= 7	14-7= 7
14-9= 5	10-2= 8	10-4= 6
8-2= 6	9-3= 6	10-4= 6
13-5= 8	10-1= 9	9-0= 9
10-0= 10	13-4= 9	13-6= 7
16-7= 9	16-9= 7	11-5= 6
15-5= 10	20-10= 10	15-9= 6

TIMED TEST #8 · 3 MINUTES
0-20 SUBTRACTION

10-3= 7	9-2= 7	8-1= 7
10-2= 8	9-1= 8	8-0= 8
13-3= 10	12-2= 10	11-1= 10
13-9= 4	12-8= 4	11-7= 4
15-9= 6	14-9= 5	13-6= 7
14-5=	13-5= 8	12-5= 7
13-4= 9	12-4= 8	11-4= 7
20-10= 10	18-9= 9	16-8= 8
14-7= 7	12-6= 6	10-5= 5
17-9= 8	16-9= 7	15-9= 6
17-8= 9	16-8= 8	15-8= 7
15-6= 9	15-7= 8	15-8= 7
12-3= 9	11-3= 8	10-3= 7
12-2= 10	11-2= 9	13-7= 6
13-3= 10	12-3= 9	7-1= 6

TIMED TEST #9 · 4 MINUTES

0-20 ADDITION & SUBTRACTION

12 − 7 = 5	12 − 8 = 4	9 + 9 = 18
8 − 4 = 4	6 + 4 = 10	11 − 4 = 7
10 − 8 = 2	8 + 4 = 12	6 + 6 = 12
11 − 9 = 2	11 − 6 = 5	9 − 7 = 2
9 + 7 = 16	9 − 4 = 5	8 − 5 = 3
10 − 2 = 8	7 + 6 = 13	11 − 8 = 3
8 + 7 = 15	12 − 6 = 6	6 + 8 = 14
20 − 5 = 15	6 + 5 = 11	2 + 3 = 5
5 + 9 = 14	11 − 2 = 9	7 + 5 = 12
2 + 6 = 8	9 + 3 = 12	12 − 9 = 3
12 − 8 = 4	9 − 5 = 4	9 + 5 = 14
4 + 8 = 12	11 − 9 = 2	9 + 4 = 13
5 − 2 = 3	8 + 3 = 11	10 − 6 = 4
8 + 8 = 16	12 − 7 = 5	2 + 8 = 10
9 − 6 = 3	9 + 8 = 17	7 − 2 = 5

TIMED TEST #10 · 3 MINUTES

0-20 ADDITION & SUBTRACTION

6 + 5 = 11	11 − 6 = 5	11 − 3 = 8
7 − 2 = 5	9 + 3 = 12	5 + 9 = 14
7 + 6 = 13	10 − 3 = 7	20 − 10 = 10
12 − 6 = 6	9 + 8 = 17	11 − 9 = 2
9 + 5 = 14	6 + 8 = 14	8 + 7 = 15
2 + 8 = 10	12 − 8 = 4	9 − 5 = 4
11 − 8 = 3	9 − 7 = 2	6 + 4 = 10
7 + 5 = 12	5 − 2 = 3	12 − 9 = 3
11 − 4 = 7	9 + 9 = 18	10 − 8 = 2
2 + 3 = 5	12 − 7 = 5	14 − 6 = 8
8 − 5 = 3	12 − 6 = 6	8 + 4 = 12
10 − 6 = 4	9 − 4 = 5	11 − 8 = 3
11 − 2 = 9	9 + 7 = 16	9 − 6 = 3
9 + 4 = 13	8 + 3 = 11	2 + 6 = 8
6 + 6 = 12	6 − 5 = 1	8 + 8 = 16

ABOUT THE AUTHOR

Naoya Imanishi, MEd, has been an educator in the Los Angeles Unified School District since 2000, serving as a third-grade teacher, math coach, and currently a school coordinator. He also works with the UCLA Mathematics Project as a teacher leader and coach for professional development in Cognitively Guided Instruction. While attaining his bachelor's and master's in education at UCLA, he was one of the first producers of LCC Theatre Company and co-founder of ProperGander, both Asian American theater companies with notable alumni. Naoya enjoys video editing, snowboarding, and cooking for his wife, Jennifer, their two sons, Kyle and Jordan, and their dog, Buddy.

ABOUT THE ILLUSTRATOR

Gareth Williams lives in London with his amazing wife. From an early age he's loved to draw, and that passion continues to this day. It's something he still can't believe he gets to do for a living. Gareth has illustrated everything from editorial illustrations to children's books. He loved working on this project and hopes you will love it just as much.

Grown-ups, you can find him on Instagram @gareth.designs

From board books to reads for teens, **Brightly** helps raise lifelong learners by celebrating the countless adventures and moments of connection that books can offer. We take pride in working with a diverse group of contributors, authors, and partners who provide a multitude of ways to cultivate a love of books and learning new skills in children of all ages.

A Brightly Book is expertly designed to provide young readers with a fun, age-appropriate, and hands-on learning experience. We hope you and your little ones enjoy this book as much as we do.

Happy reading!

See all that Brightly has to offer at **readbrightly.com**.